MW00423275

Read
Write
Code

A FRIENDLY INTRODUCTION
TO THE WORLD OF CODING, AND
WHY IT'S THE NEW LITERACY

Jeremy Keeshin

LIONCREST
PUBLISHING

READ WRITE CODE
*A Friendly Introduction to the World of Coding,
and Why It's the New Literacy*

ISBN   978-1-5445-1799-5 *Hardcover*
       978-1-5445-1798-8 *Paperback*
       978-1-5445-1797-1 *Ebook*

*To my parents, for encouraging me to be
curious and answering many years of
"How does this work?" and "Why?" questions.*

Contents

0
Introduction

100101010110100010101010001010100)01001010101010101010101111010101100101010010101010100101010010101

What is code?

How does the internet work?

What does it mean when something gets hacked? Should you be worried about Google tracking your data or facial recognition algorithms? Will artificial intelligence replace your job? What even *is* Bitcoin? How does someone make an app or a website? What is a database? Where is the cloud?

And how do these questions all fit together?

For many people, when they hear something about technology or code, everything sounds like mumbo jumbo and gobbledygook. This book is here to help unscramble that feeling for you.

You can understand all this. And in this day and age, you really don't have an option not to. Understanding code is crucial to understanding our modern world.

It's hard to predict the future. But there's a clear trend that isn't going away anytime soon. Technology and the code that creates it are increasingly influencing and changing our society. Coding is a new foundational skill, just like reading and writing.

It can be intimidating, but if you want to make sense of the world of coding, you've come to the right place.

There are many components that make up the digital systems we have today, and you may be overwhelmed, confused, or even lost as to where to start.

This book is like a map. It will explain coding to you in

simple terms, walk you through the parts, and show you how it all connects.

You'll learn what code is and how it works. You'll understand how you get from the apps on your phone to the hardware it runs on. You'll understand how the internet works and how we get from 0s and 1s that make up the digital world to the algorithms and cloud that power modern technology. You'll learn cybersecurity basics and how to think about artificial intelligence.

If you want to keep learning, you'll discover lots of ways to learn more. If you want to understand how coding applies to your life, you'll have many practical ideas you can walk away with. It's no small thing to unlock the mysteries of the digital world.

My name is Jeremy, and I'm the CEO and co-founder of CodeHS. We have taught millions of students coding and computer science through our site, and we have 20,000 classrooms of students and teachers that use our site each month. I studied computer science and artificial intelligence at Stanford and taught the introductory computer science courses there. I now have direct experience working with thousands of teachers and schools and have visited hundreds of classrooms for computer science around the country and around the world.

Lots of places can explain coding and technology to you in a complicated way. What's hard is explaining it in a simple way—in a way that a middle schooler or high schooler will understand but also in a way that an adult who just wants to get it will appreciate.

Read Write Code—A New Foundational Skill

Reading and writing are foundational skills that we expect students to learn and adults to know. It's part of basic literacy and crucial to being able to contribute to day-to-day life as an active citizen.

We expect people to know how to read and write, but you don't need to become a professional reader or a professional writer to find those skills useful. You're going to read all the time and write all the time, whether that is to understand a news article or to write an email. They are foundational skills.

Now that we live in a technology-driven world, coding is a new foundational skill. As technology impacts and fundamentally alters every industry and society, understanding how code works is crucial to being digitally literate.

Today, we see reading and writing as crucial skills. But that wasn't always the case. Go back 500 years and reading and writing were skills reserved only for the elite. Most people didn't think they needed reading and writing. But if you did know how to read and write, it opened up a whole new world of opportunities. Then, with the invention of the printing press, reading and writing transformed literacy and society.

Gutenberg created the printing press around 1440; then, in the next century, 200 million copies were printed. This laid the groundwork for the Scientific Revolution, the Enlightenment, and then massive increases in literacy from 1600–1800 in Europe. What's now obvious—the usefulness of literacy, of being able to read and write—was not a thing in 1400. But there was a tectonic shift with the printing press—with literacy—and we see how this new access to information changed society and education.

The changes brought about by Gutenberg and the printing press are analogous to where we are today with code, computers, and the internet.

Now, with the invention of computers and the rise of the internet, we are at the tipping point of this same trend. Most people don't know coding or see how it is useful to them. There is a small group of people who do know how to code and have access to the opportunity it presents. Coding is to computers and the internet as reading and writing are to the printing press—crucial new skills enabled by transformative and society-shifting technology. We're in the year 1500 for computers.

How to Read This Book

The best way to read this book is to try things out along the way. You'll see sections labeled "Try It," and in each of those sections, you can try out a program, run the code, or explore an idea interactively.

Make sure to visit the website that goes along with this book at *readwritecodebook.com*. It's full of interactive coding examples you can try that are all organized by chapter, so you can easily find the right example. You can try existing programs, and you'll also have a chance to write your own new programs. Seeing the code in action and testing it out will help things make more sense.

This book isn't going to make you a professional programmer. It's not going to make you a coding wizard. But it will give you a solid foundation of the basics. If you want to understand what coding is and why it matters today, then this book is for you.

Are you ready to demystify the world of coding? Let's dive in.

1
Hello World

Hello world! That's often the first line of code that people write when they learn a new programming language—it's a tradition now. It's also a way to say hello and welcome to this book.

So, what is code? What is coding?

Coding is giving instructions to a computer. **Code** is the instructions for the computer.

What does code look like? How do you write it? Where does it go?

If you've never heard of coding, there is a long list of questions to even find out where to start.

Here's a line of code:

```
print("Hello")
```

That's code that prints out the word "Hello" to the screen in the programming language Python. You can write code to do that in all sorts of ways.

```
printf("Hello");
```

This is how you write code to print "Hello" to the screen in the C programming language. In Java, you might write:

```
System.out.println("Hello");
```

But code does a lot more than print. Code is really the set of instructions that makes technology go. When you type an email and hit send, someone has written code to make that work. When you open your phone, hit an icon that looks like a camera, and take a photo, and it saves to the cloud—that is code. People write code to create software. There's a whole invisible world of code that we are going to explore in this book.

It also is a superpower—it lets you leverage the power of technology in all sorts of creative ways.

If you want an easy way to see what code looks like (this would be HTML, CSS, and JavaScript), go to any web page, right-click, and then select "View Page Source." That's the code that created the web page.

Programming Languages

A **programming language** is the specific "language" or set of rules for giving instructions to a computer. There are many different programming languages used for different things. Some become more popular or less popular over time. They are built for different use cases and have different tradeoffs.

Spoken languages are a very loose analogy to programming languages: the languages all let you communicate but have different words, phrases, or approaches. Unlike a spoken language, like Spanish or French, you wouldn't really say that you "speak" a programming language. You could say that you write that language or can code or program in it. You could say that you understand it. But you don't really speak programming languages.

Programming languages are related, they have different histories and taxonomies, they evolve over time, and, in that way, they are similar to foreign languages.

A few examples of programming languages are JavaScript, Python, C, C++, and Java. There are many, many more!

There are **domain-specific languages**—meaning a programming language that's really good for a particular type of task. For example, SQL is used specifically for databases, and MATLAB is used specifically for mathematical data and scientific modeling.

C is a popular programming language that inspired a family of languages, such as Java, JavaScript, C++, and many more. These share a similar syntax and a number of other related ideas.

Many programmers can get very intense—almost religious—about their preferences in programming languages. That's not really a fact about programming languages, more an observation about some of the community behavior around it.

Software, Apps, and Programs

There are a lot of coding-related words. Some of them mean specific things, some of them mean overlapping things, and it can get hard to keep track of them. Throughout the book, I'll introduce some of those key words and how they all relate to each other.

So, the first is code. **Code** is the actual instructions being run by a computer. It's also fair to refer to a collection of code in its entirety as a **computer program** or just a **program**. If you write a program, you could also call that program **software**. It's also accurate to call a piece of software an **application**, and **app** is just short for application.

Okay, so this is confusing. Does this mean that code, program, software, and app are all kind of the same thing? It kind of does. The thing to note about each of these words is they each happen to have different connotations and are used in different ways.

For example, you may be familiar with apps in the context of mobile apps, like iPhone apps and Android apps. A **mobile app** is really just a computer program that runs on a phone. A **web app** is a program that runs on the web, or the internet. And a **desktop app** is a program that runs on your computer. An app, or application, can really refer to anything in this category. So, people may use "app" as shorthand to mean "mobile app," but it's more technically correct that you could refer to any software as an application.

In many instances, "app," "program," and "software" can be used interchangeably. The code is what you are actually writing to build the app. "App" has more of a user-facing use case, while "program" or "code" is the terminology used more by the creators of the software.

Hello World, Again

Hello world, again. Now that you have a few important words and ideas, let's revisit Hello World again.

So, Hello World is, by tradition, typically one of the first programs people write in a new programming language they are learning. The idea is that to test out that new language, first, see if you can print the words "Hello world" to the screen. It's often just a few lines of code to write the Hello World program.

So, we'll start with a programming language called Python.

Here is Hello World in Python:

```
print("Hello world")
```

That's it! Nice and easy. Just one line of code. If you want to try running this program, open up your Terminal program (if you have a Mac) and then type:

```
python
```

Then enter. And then type the next line exactly as it appears:

```
print("Hello world")
```

Be careful to make sure you include the quote and paren-theses. When you program, the computer can get very picky. But that's it! Now, say you want to write it in JavaScript. JavaScript is the programming language of the browser. In JavaScript, you can write Hello world like this:

```
console.log("Hello world");
```

To run this one, open up your web browser, like Google Chrome. Then, go to *google.com*. Right-click and select "Inspect." Click "Console" and type:

```
console.log("Hello world");
```

In Java, it gets a little more complicated:

```
public class HelloWorld {
    public static void main(String[] args) {
        System.out.println("Hello world");
    }
}
```

What's nice about the Hello World program is that it gives you a bit of insight into the patterns of the language. There are already a few patterns we can spot.

One is that in each program, we wrote "Hello world" in between quotes. That's called a **string**, and it's something that is common to Python, Java, and JavaScript.

I see another pattern, which is that Java and JavaScript end some of the lines with semicolons (;), while Python doesn't.

I can also see that the "Hello world" is written between parentheses.

How do you write Hello World in the Ruby programming language? In Ruby, you write:

```
puts "Hello world"
```

Which one is that most like?

In the language C, Hello World looks like:

```
#include <stdio.h>
int main()
{
  printf("Hello world");
  return 0;
}
```

In C++, Hello World looks like:

```
#include <iostream>
int main()
{
    std::cout << "Hello world" << endl;
    return 0;
}
```

You can see that C and C++ look pretty similar but are a little different. In C, it uses the word `printf`, and in C++, it uses the line `std::cout` (though in C++, you can also use `printf` since it supports a lot of that same functionality). It's pretty crazy to see how much you can learn just from writing this simple program.

Printing Out Hello World by Language

Language	Code to Print Hello World
Python	`print("Hello world")`
JavaScript	`console.log("Hello world")`
Ruby	`puts "Hello world"`
Java	`System.out.println("Hello world");`
C++	`std::cout << "Hello world" << endl;`
C	`printf("Hello world");`

Write Your First Program

The best way to learn to code is to try it out. Visit the website for this book at *readwritecodebook.com*, and you can try running all of these Hello World programs. While you are there, try this:

- Run Hello World in Python
- Run Hello World in JavaScript
- Run Hello World in C++
- Run Hello World in Java
- Try changing the text that gets printed out

Assembly Language and Machine Code

So, you can look at things from top-down or bottom-up. Top-down often means working at the highest levels, something that is most easily understood by a human, and going down. The low level languages are things that are closest to the actual hardware or, really, closest to just being 1s and 0s.

So, if earlier we were writing in a human-readable programming language like Python or JavaScript, that is considered high level. Sometimes languages are split into higher-level and lower-level languages, depending on what features they give you access to.

Assembly language is one of the lowest-level languages. It's often what a program gets converted into on the way between being written by a person and being run by a computer.

Assembly language has a simpler set of very basic instructions. These include instructions like moving a number from one place to another. It also has instructions for adding numbers. There are other mathematical instructions and logical operators. There are also commands for program flow, like those to call a function or jump to another part of a program.

Here's what an assembly code instruction might be like to move a number to a different location:

```
mov eax, 7h
```

This instruction moves the hexadecimal number 7 to the register **eax**. Here, register **eax** is just a particular location on the computer that is easily accessible.

Mainly, it's very hard to write complicated programs in a language like this. But this is what the computer is doing at a very low level. There's even a lower level, which is called **machine code**, which is run directly by the computer and is just numbers.

Compilers and Interpreters

So, while it seems as simple as just writing "`print(10)`" to the screen and then it just works, there's a lot that happens in the middle.

This work is done by something called the **compiler**. The compiler **compiles**, or turns a program in one language into a program in another language. The compiler is itself a computer program, and the way it normally works is it turns a higher-level language into a lower-level language. So, it might turn your C program or Java program into something that can be run by a computer.

So, the way it works with a compiler is:

1. Write a program
2. Compile the program
3. Compiler generates another program
4. Run the resulting program

Many languages are compiled, but some are interpreted. An interpreter essentially tries to run it right away. So, an **interpreter** uses these steps:

1. Write a program
2. Run a program in an interpreter

Python and JavaScript, which are considered **scripting languages**, are also interpreted. Java and C, for example, are **compiled languages**.

Operating Systems

What operating system are you running? If you use a Mac, it might be Mac OS, Mac OSX, or iOS—the OS here stands for "operating system." If you were running a PC, or some laptop or desktop from Microsoft, then you might be running the Windows operating system. If you are familiar with open source, you might be running Linux or a particular Linux distribution like Ubuntu. Android is an operating system for mobile phones.

You might have heard the names of some operating systems and know that you use one, but what even is an operating system? That is a very good question. There are many common features of operating systems, and they all vary quite a bit, but at the simplest level, the **operating system** is the low-level software that actually makes the computer go. It works with the hardware and controls tasks like managing the memory, allowing programs to run, getting user input, and a number of other things.

The operating system is the software that sits between some application, like your web browser, and the actual hardware. You can think of it like this: You have a computer or a phone, which just starts as hardware. That hardware isn't quite usable yet. If you want to start to send a text message or visit a web page—that's an application—how does that application run directly on the hardware? What actually happens is there is software in between—the operating system—that handles some basic and common tasks that are needed to run lots of types of applications. And then, it provides a way for applications to be written on top of it. So, an iPhone developer, Android program-mer, or any mobile developer is building their app on top of the phone operating system.

Fitting It All Together

So, how does this all fit together? Well, at the highest level, I'm using my computer right now, typing on my keyboard, and using Google Docs. Using some of this new vocabulary and understanding, how can we understand this a bit more?

Google Docs is a software application running in my web browser, Google Chrome, which is also a software application. Chrome, the web browser, is a native applica-tion running on the Mac OS operating system.

When I type a key, I'm actually interacting with the hardware—the keyboard. When I type, that sends a signal, and the operating system gets an **interrupt**, meaning an indication that something just happened. And then, that information is passed back into the web browser and web application.

At another level, there is code written for Google Docs, in JavaScript, that is running on my computer in my web browser. That code is being interpreted and run, going from the instructions the programmers wrote to actually being in a language the computer can understand.

And at another level, Google Chrome is written in another language, C++, which is then compiled into an executable program (the Google Chrome app), which, when I click on it, runs the application (also known as a binary!).

So, there is a lot, lot more here. But you can see a bit of what is going on, how code makes software, how applications are software, and how applications can run on operating systems. And not only that, we have code that turns programs into other programs, which is what compilers do. It's a bit mind-bending.

From the Abacus to the iPhone

Today, you can have a supercomputer in your pocket in the form of a smartphone. Today, a new iPhone 11 is 6 inches by 3 inches, can have 256GB of storage, make calls, access the web, take photos and videos, and run all sorts of software apps.

We've come a long way from the early computers. What was the first computer? That's a hard question. But there have been tools for a long time to help with computations, though it has accelerated in the last fifty (and especially the last twenty) years.

The earliest known computing device is the abacus, which appeared as early as 2300 BC and was an early tool for calculations.

Skip forward a few thousand years, and in 1801, Joseph Marie Jacquard created a loom that used punch cards to create repeatable designs.

Later in 1822, Charles Babbage, a mathematician and inventor, created the idea of a calculating device, the Difference Engine. Later, he invented the Analytical Engine, which had many elements of computers today, though it was never built.

Ada Lovelace, who was friends with and worked with Charles Babbage, extended these ideas on the Analytical Engine to show how it could be used beyond calculations, devised an algorithm for computing Bernoulli numbers, and is considered the first programmer.

In 1936, Alan Turing created the idea of a general computer, a Turing Machine.

In 1945, ENIAC was completed, which was the first general-purpose digital computer and cost about $6.5 million in today's dollars, weighed thirty tons, and occupied 1,800 square feet.

In the 1960s, large mainframe computers became more common, and the mouse and graphical interface were introduced. In the 1970s, personal computers became more readily available. The first call on a cell phone was made in 1973, and the phone weighed two kilograms and cost over $1 million in today's dollars. Fast forward, and the first iPhone was released in 2007.

Since the 1970s, computers have evolved rapidly and become smaller and faster to the proliferation of devices we have today. The ENIAC could do 5,000 addition operations per second and 385 multiplication operations per second. A modern iPhone, which is a fraction of the size, has a processor with a speed of 2.66 billion cycles per second and can do hundreds of billions of operations in a second.

Brief History of Computers Timeline

Year	Computer
2300 BC	Abacus
1801	Jacquard Loom
1822	Difference Engine
1837	Analytical Engine
1936	Turing Machine
1945	ENIAC
1960s	Mainframe Computers
1970s	Personal Computers
1973	First Cell Phone
2007	First iPhone

Bugs and Debugging

Writing code is giving instructions to a computer—sounds like it should be simple, right? Turns out it's often very complex, despite good ideas around how to break down problems. When there is an error in your code or your software, it's called a **bug**. Fixing those errors and tracking them down is called **debugging**.

Debugging code is like being a detective. Something isn't going quite right, and you need to find out the source of the error. You'll have to use the output of the program, any symptoms you can find along the way, and a number of tools you have at your disposal to track them down. To debug problems, programmers can track the flow of the program, find out what the program does at each step, and try to examine where they went wrong—and maybe most importantly, question their assumptions about how things are working.

Bugs can be really tricky. And surprising. And simple. Ask someone who has programmed for a while about a difficult bug. A big bug in a complex system can arise from a small typo, a missing quote or semicolon, or switching a word. Sometimes things are working, and you don't change the code, and then something stops working! How could that be? That sometimes happens when you get a new set of input data or an edge case, or something else about the system could change. An **edge case** is some extreme test case you didn't consider when writing your program.

For example, let's say you were writing a program to divide two numbers. And you get your program to work. And you test it out on a wide range of numbers. Then, you give your program to a friend who tries to divide by zero, and your program breaks or crashes. You weren't expecting anyone to ever think of trying to divide by zero! They tested an edge case and found a bug. And now you have to go find what was wrong and debug it.

It turns out programs are really buggy. There are bugs all the time. There isn't really a system that is just "done" or just works. A website you use every day may have tons of crashes and bugs behind the scenes. Not every bug stops the entire functioning of a program.

But software always has bugs. So, things can work pretty well, even when they are broken. As you uncover the complexity and inner workings of code and computers, sometimes it's surprising that everything works.

Some Really Bad Bugs

Some bugs aren't so bad. In the bug in our division program that didn't handle dividing by zero, it seems like everything will be okay, and you can take the time to go and fix the program so that it handles that input. But what if that divide-by-zero bug was part of a larger program?

Some bugs are really bad. And have huge impacts. And they may have started from a simple issue.

More recently, bugs have gotten more prominent and ominous-sounding names and been in the news. In 2018, there were two vulnerabilities—or, really, bugs—named "Spectre" and "Meltdown," which happened because there were issues at the chip level in very common hardware.

In 2002, there was a study from the US Department of Commerce that found bugs cost the US economy $59 billion annually.

There was a famous bug in 1982 with the Therac-25 radiation machine where patients could get radiation doses hundreds of times greater than normal, which resulted in many deaths. That was a very bad bug.

In 1962, the Mariner I rocket heading to Venus crashed five minutes in because of a missing line—yes, this is true. It was an $80 million project then, equaling $685 million in 2020 dollars. It was called the "most expensive hyphen in history"—though it was an overbar (¯), not a hyphen (-).

Some people might remember the "Y2K Bug," or the Year 2000 Bug. This was a bug related to the formatting of dates. Many computers just stored the last two digits of dates, so 1993 would just be 93. This meant that you couldn't tell the difference between the years 2000 and 1900.

So, when you use programs: sometimes, if it's not working, it might be you, but many times there might be a bug in the code.

2
It's All Zeros and Ones

Y2K Bug

In January 1999, the cover of *Time* magazine declared "The End of The World" with the Y2K Bug. The year 2000 was approaching, and there was about to be a big issue. Computers, which had been working just fine up until then, had a problem. The date was often stored with only two numbers to represent the year, like 95 for 1995. So, when the year 1999 turned to 2000, and 99 became 00—was that 1900 or 2000? Or something else? Would everything break and reset? What would happen to the banks? Would the digital world collapse?

To understand the Y2K Bug, or Year 2000 Bug, you'll want to know what is going on under the hood with computers and how numbers are represented and interpreted. Why didn't they just use more digits to store the dates and avoid this problem? Well, early on, the storage was expensive, so people took shortcuts like this.

It's estimated that $300 billion was spent to prep and fix bugs due to Y2K, or $426 billion in today's dollars. Who would think that the way you choose to represent dates could have so many repercussions or cause so many problems? To understand that, it's helpful to see how information is represented and stored in computers.

Binary—It's All 1s and 0s

This is one of my favorite concepts—that everything on computers is really all just 1s and 0s. You may work with a programming language or an application or see an image or a video, but as you go down deeper and deeper to understand how this all works, you see that everything is 1s and 0s.

The system for everything being 1s and 0s is called **binary**.

Binary is a base-2 number system, meaning you can write any number and express it as a combination of 1s and 0s. A number system you may be more familiar with is the **base-10**, or **decimal**, **number system**. That means a number like:

352

means three hundred and fifty-two. However, another way to think about that number is that there are:

3   one hundreds
5   tens
2   ones

This is how you may have learned about numbers when you were younger. However, if you break that down a bit more, you'll find that each "place"—the "ones place," the "tens place," the "hundreds place," etc.—is really a power of ten.

This means the reason the ones place is first is that one is equal to 10^0 (ten to the zeroth power or 10^0). The second one is the tens place, which is 10^1 (ten to the first power or 10^1), and then the third one is the hundreds place, or 10^2 (ten to the second power), or 10 x 10, which is 100.

Another way to look at that is with this table:

	3	5	2
Place	100s place	10s place	1s place
Power of 10	$10^2 = 100$	$10^1 = 10$	$10^0 = 1$
Result	3 x 100 = 300	5 x 10 = 50	2 x 1 = 2

So: 300 + 50 + 2 = 352.

This is more familiar in base-10.

Now, in base-2, or binary, it all works the same way, except the places are the powers of 2, not the powers of 10. The thing that makes this a bit tricky is that we are more naturally used to the powers of ten, and not as much used to the powers of 2.

So instead of 1s, 10s, 100s, 1000s, like in base-10, in base-2, it is 1s, 2s, 4s, 8s, etc. The reasons it's 1s, 2s, 4s, and 8s is because those are the powers of 2. The first power of 2 is 2^0 = 1. The second is 2^1 = 2. The third is 2^2 = 4.

The other part of base-10 is you have 10 options for what the digit can be, which is the numbers 0, 1, 2, 3, 4, 5, 6, 7, 8, and 9.

However, in base-2, you have the powers of 2 as the places, but only two options—the numbers 0 and 1 as the digits.

Say you have the binary number **101**:

	1	0	1
Place	4s place	2s place	1s place
Power of 2	$2^2 = 4$	$2^1 = 2$	$2^0 = 1$
Result	$1 \times 4 = 4$	$0 \times 2 = 0$	$1 \times 1 = 1$

$4 + 0 + 1 = 5$

So, 101 in binary is equal to 5 in base-10.

Now what is crazy about binary and base-2 for computers is everything is 1s and 0s all the way at the bottom. Even the most advanced high-definition movie.

Now, how might you get there? Well, a movie might be made up of images. And each image might be made up of pixels (single-colored dots). And each pixel is made up of a red, green, and blue component. And each red, green, and blue component is represented as a number from 0–255, which is 1 byte, or 8 bits. Or a number between **00000000** and **11111111**.

So, the way computers are working, ultimately, is everything somehow is encoded or turned into binary data. There is some representation that makes your website a long list of binary numbers. But this is true for every data type. The reason that binary data is so important and powerful is that there's an interesting feature of it just being 1s and 0s. 1 and 0 can be very easily mapped to the ideas of "on and off" or "true and false." And those are the parts that build up computers called transistors.

TRY IT

Convert a Binary Number

Can you figure out what this binary number is? What would each of these numbers be in base-10?

First, try: 110
Then, try: 10101
Then, try: 10011101

Binary to Bits to Bytes to Megabytes and Gigabytes

Now you've learned binary. Binary is the base-2 numbering system. Binary is just numbers that only have 1s and 0s. The little trick about binary is that you can interpret the binary in many, many different ways.

10010 is a binary number. So is 11011101101. You can really write any number as a binary number.

A single 1 or 0 in binary is called a **bit**, which is a combination of "binary" and "digit"—so a bit is a binary digit.

Now, people have come up with lots of ways to refer to bits. There's a word for a long list of bits in a row—**bitstring**.

There are a few more special words to know. When you have 8 bits, that's called a **byte**. Why is that? It was a deliberate misspelling of "bite," so it didn't get confused with "bit."

You may have heard of a few of these other terms—when you take the metric system prefixes and add them on to byte—like giga- or mega- or kilo-. Kilometer means 1,000 meters because the kilo- prefix means 1,000. **Kilobyte** means 1,000 bytes. The mega prefix means 1,000,000 or 10^6, so **megabyte** means 1 million bytes. And **gigabyte** means 1,000,000,000 or 1 billion bytes, or 10^9. The reason you might find some discrepancies in some cases is since computers are more natural with powers of 2, they may use the closest power of 2 instead of the closest power of 10. So, a megabyte may be 2^20 bits or 1,048,576, which is still close to 1 million.

When I visited *google.com*, my computer downloaded 520 kilobytes (kB) or 520 × 1,000 bytes, or 520,000 bytes, or 4,160,000 bits. It's kind of crazy that your computer can get 4 million 1s and 0s so quickly transferred from the other side of the world. If you download a song, that may be a few (maybe 2–3) megabytes. That means it takes 3 ×

1 million bytes, or 3 × 8 million bits, or 24 million bits to represent a song.

A movie might be 1–2 gigabytes (shortened as GB). That's 1 billion bytes, or 8 billion bits. So, a 2GB movie is 16 billion 1s and 0s. Yup.

Now, there is another place you may have heard this, which is your internet speed. While lots of things are referred to in bytes—megabytes and gigabytes—your internet speed is often referred to in bits—mega*bits* and giga*bits*. So, when people use "byte," they often write a capital B—**GB** means "gigabytes." But the term "bits" is abbreviated with a lowercase b. So, "megabits" is **Mb**. When I run a speed test, I get 68 Mbps (megabits per second) download and 34 Mbps upload.

TRY IT
Gigabytes to Bits

Here's a question: how much data can be stored on your computer? My current computer has a capacity of 500GB. How many bits is that?

Test your own internet speed by visiting *fast.com*. How many bits per second is that?

Okay, now we can find out what that means. 68 Mbps means I get 68 million bits per second downloaded to my computer. And I can send out—or upload—34 million bits per second from my computer. That means my download speed in bytes is 8.5 million bytes per second. (I divided 68 by 8 bits in a byte.) So, I should be able to download a couple of songs in a second.

Images and Pixels

How do images and videos work on computers? To understand this, we'll use some of the same principles that repeatedly appear throughout computer science, which is breaking things down into smaller problems (or **problem decomposition**) and abstraction.

The first thing to do is imagine that you have a color-by-number book. And you have the number 1, which represents purple, and 2 represents blue, and so on. You can go and fill in the page, coloring purple where you see a 1, and blue where you see a 2, and as you fill in the colors, you create an image. Here, our color-by-number image will create a bird.

Your color-by-number book may not have many restrictions; the areas that you color could be all sorts of shapes and curves. What if we made a small modification, and we created the rule that the only shape that we could have is a small square? So, our color-by-number exercise

1 - purple   2 - blue   3 - light blue   4 - dark green
5 - green   6 - yellow   7 - orange   8 - brown   9 - red

is really now more like a grid. In our image of the fox, 1 is black, 2 is orange, and 3 is blue. But each element in the color-by-number image is a small square.

COLOR BY NUMBERS

Now, when we color in all the squares, we still get a nice colorful fox image. The difference is, when we create the restriction that the only shapes allowed are square, we've made it much more general-purpose. The way images on computers work is exactly this way. And there is a name for each of the squares in the image, which is a pixel.

The word **pixel** is a combination of the word picture and element, so it's a picture element. A pixel is the smallest element in a digital image. Another way to think of it is just a single colored dot on an image.

So, say you take an image file, maybe a JPG or PNG file, and zoom in. Before you zoom in, it looks just like a regular image. It doesn't look like there are lots of small dots. But when you zoom in and zoom in, you see that it actually looks more like our color-by-number example from before.

The next image is a zoomed-out photo from Bali.

As you zoom in more and more, you can see the image is starting to get "pixelated," where we can see the actual dots.

If I keep zooming in more and more and more, I'll see something like the image on the following page.

And you can see that an image is just a collection of colored dots or squares, just like the color-by-number example above. Digital images are all just collections of pixels.

Zoom In to See Pixels

Take an image that you have on your
computer. Download it if it is an image from
online. Now try to zoom in and then keep
zooming in until you can see the individual
pixels. On a Mac, if I open an image in the
Preview app, I can click "View," then "Zoom
In," or use the keyboard shortcut command +.

What's a Pixel? Red, Green, Blue

An image is just a grid of pixels. And a pixel is just a colored dot. What's nice about digital images, compared to drawing by hand, is you can have a lot more colors.

How do you generate a color? How do you actually pick the specific color of that dot, or pixel?

You choose it by setting a red, green, and blue value. The reason it is red, green, and blue is that these are the three primary colors of light, meaning you can combine them in different amounts to get any color.

So, say we want a red pixel; how do we get that?

Well, to get a pixel that is all red, we just want the full red component, but we don't want any green or blue.

The amount of red is specified by a number between 0 and 255 (256 options). Why 256? Well, it turns out that 256 is 2^8 (2 to the 8th power), or the number of options you can represent with 8 bits, or 1 byte! You'll see the numbers 255 and 256 popping up a lot. (Notice, with code, we usually start counting at 0.)

To get the full red color, we want red at 255, then blue at 0, and green at 0.

And that is actually how you get red. Oftentimes, for colors, people represent them with a **hexadecimal** (base-16) shorthand, meaning they use the hexadecimal versions of the numbers 0–255. So, 0 in hex (short for hexadecimal) is still 0, but 255 is FF. So, the color for red is written like:

Explore Hexadecimal Colors

So, you can create almost any color just with six hexadecimal digits. Here's a particular type of orange: #f2a84b, and here are the red, green, and blue components: (242, 168, 75). You can try it out at the website for this book on the examples for this chapter (*readwritecodebook.com*).

One thing that you can do to explore this is use the "eyedropper" tool available in many image editing programs or your web browser. If you are in Photoshop or Illustrator, click the eyedropper tool and select a color; it will make it your current color. Then, if you click on that color, you can see that it will show the hex value!

#FF0000

Say we want a yellow-colored pixel. How do we get that? To get yellow, we combine red and green. Remember, here, we are combining colors and mixing light. Not mixing paint.

If we want equal parts red and green and no blue, we want 255 red, 255 green, and 0 blue.

That would be:

Yellow = (255, 255, 0)

In hexadecimal:

Yellow = #FFFF00

This one is a bit trickier, but if you go into your console on your web browser (right-click and select "Inspect"), and you select text or anything with a color, you'll see a little color box. If you double-click that, it will pull up a color picker and show you the hexadecimal values.

Encodings

Representing colors with computers—which are actually three red, green, and blue components, which can be represented with six hexadecimal characters, which really are binary numbers—is an example of using encodings. **Encoding** is a way to take some data and represent it in a different format. We can encode colors, numbers, letters, or really anything.

That's what's going on with computers—at the bottom, it's all 1s and 0s. But we can put together those 1s and 0s in different ways. Often, the first thing to build up from 1s and 0s is numbers. Then, from those numbers, we can make colors. Or from those numbers, we can make letters or words.

So, with colors, the encoding could be understood as:

A color → red, green, blue components → RGB hex value → underlying bitstring

This means that, at each step, it's the same information, just represented in a different format. Take a look at the values in the table; these all mean the same thing.

Color	Red
RGB, decimal	(255, 0, 0)
RGB, hexadecimal	#FF0000
RGB, binary	11111111 00000000 00000000

Say you are encoding an image; the sequence taking you from the image to the binary data might look like:

Image → grid or list of pixels → red, green, and blue components → RGB hex values → binary data

Characters and Strings:
How Do Computers Make Words?

We've talked a little bit about how you can go from bits to numbers and from bits to colors and images. Now, how do you go from bits to words?

Before we get to words, we need to take one step in between and get to letters. So, in most code lingo, letters are referred to as **characters**. They are represented differently in different languages, but there is a surprising amount of complexity just to represent letters.

There are twenty-six letters in English, but there are also lowercase and uppercase letters.

Considering that storing things with computers starts with 1s and 0s, what if we made letters and words like this:

We'll start with 1s and 0s—in binary. And then, we'll create a list of numbers; we can even think of those numbers in decimal. What if we match each of those numbers to represent a letter? This is exactly how one encoding system works: the ASCII character encoding.

To make a word, what we'll do is put the information for each letter right next to each other.

Say we had a simple alphabet with just the letters A, B,

C, and D.

Say we use 2 bits to represent this language since 2^2 (base-2 for binary, and the power is 2 for 2 bits) = 4 letters.

Encoding	Character
00	A
01	B
10	C
11	D

So, now, we have an encoding table for our language! What letter is this?

```
10
```

That's a C.

What word is this?

```
100001
```

To break it down, we'll only look at 2 bits at a time since each letter is two bits.

```
10  00  01
```

If we look those up in our table, we see this is the word:

C   A   B

And this is a pretty good approximation of how computers make letters and words. There is a unique binary encoding that is matched to a letter.

ASCII Chart

The **ASCII encoding** is a standard encoding for text—or characters and strings. ASCII stands for American Standard Code for Information Interchange. You can see a sample of the ASCII encoding in the provided table (see page 41).

What you can see in the table is a number on the left (in base-10) and a character on the right. You can see here that the ASCII code for capital A is 65. What's the number that encodes a lowercase f? 102. You can see capital English letters from 65 until 90, and lowercase letters go from 97 to 122.

If I had the numbers:

72 69 89

What word is that?

The following page has a small part of the ASCII table, but also showing the number in binary and hexadecimal as well.

ASCII ENCODING

Dec	Char	Dec	Char	Dec	Char	Dec	Char	Dec	Char	Dec	Char	Dec	Char	Dec	Char
0	NUL	16	DLE	32	SPC	48	0	64	@	80	P	96	`	112	p
1	SOH	17	DC1	33	!	49	1	65	A	81	Q	97	a	113	q
2	STX	18	DC2	34	"	50	2	66	B	82	R	98	b	114	r
3	ETX	19	DC3	35	#	51	3	67	C	83	S	99	c	115	s
4	EOT	20	DC4	36	$	52	4	68	D	84	T	100	d	116	t
5	ENQ	21	NAK	37	%	53	5	69	E	85	U	101	e	117	u
6	ACK	22	SYN	38	&	54	6	70	F	86	V	102	f	118	v
7	BEL	23	ETB	39	'	55	7	71	G	87	W	103	g	119	w
8	BS	24	CAN	40	(	56	8	72	H	88	X	104	h	120	x
9	HT	25	EM	41	)	57	9	73	I	89	Y	105	i	121	y
10	LF	26	SUB	42	*	58	:	74	J	90	Z	106	j	122	z
11	VT	27	ESC	43	+	59	;	75	K	91	[	107	k	123	{
12	FF	28	FS	44	,	60	<	76	L	92	\	108	l	124	|
13	CR	29	GS	45	-	61	=	77	M	93	]	109	m	125	}
14	SO	30	RS	46	.	62	>	78	N	94	^	110	n	126	~
15	SI	31	US	47	/	63	?	79	O	95	_	111	o	127	DEL

Decimal	Hex	Binary	ASCII
97	61	01100001	a
98	62	01100010	b
99	63	01100011	c
100	64	01100100	d
101	65	01100101	e
102	66	01100110	f
103	67	01100111	g
104	68	01101000	h
105	69	01101001	i
106	6A	01101010	j
107	6B	01101011	k
108	6C	01101100	l

What you can see is that each row is a different representation of the same thing. For example, 103 in decimal is the same as 67 in hexadecimal, 01100111 in binary, and g in ASCII.

While ASCII is a popular encoding, it's just one of many possible ways to encode binary numbers as characters and strings. There are some shortcomings of ASCII that you may wonder about.

ASCII only handles English characters, but you may want to represent letters in other languages or other symbols, or even emojis.

TRY IT
Mystery Word

If I had the bits:

01100010 01100101 01101100 01101100

What word is that? First, try yourself by
looking up the corresponding letter in the
table.
    The answer is "bell."

How Does a Computer Represent Emojis?

The ASCII encoding only handles a basic set of English
characters. What if we wanted to represent letters in lots
of other languages? We'd need another encoding system.
The standard encoding system for encoding text across
many languages is called **Unicode**. The latest version of
Unicode has 136,755 characters in 139 different languages.
So, it's a lot bigger than ASCII.

Unicode is a standard for the encodings; UTF-8 or UTF-
16 are some example encodings that implement this standard. **UTF-8** is the main encoding for the web, used in
over 90 percent of web pages. One interesting fact is the

start of the UTF-8 encoding table is the same as the ASCII table, so they can be compatible.

In the section for this chapter on the book website (*readwritecodebook.com*), you can explore the UTF-8 character map or Unicode characters by code points.

Try searching 1F300, and you'll see the spiral emoji, which is my favorite emoji.

So, this brings us to the question—how do computers represent emojis? Well, we need an encoding. The encoding standard is Unicode, and a popular implementation of that encoding is UTF-8. In Unicode, there is an idea of "code points." A **code point** is an in-between layer and number to represent a more abstract idea of a character. The reason for code points as a standard mapping from characters to numbers, is that there may be alternate ways of mapping from numbers to bits. UTF-8 is one way of doing it with 8 bits, but there is also UTF-16 as an alternate encoding.

So, the way computers store emojis is:

Emoji → code point → hexadecimal data → binary data

Emojis are still binary, still 1s and 0s. But there are a few ways in between of interpreting it.

If you want the regular smiling emoji, that has code point U+1F600. In UTF-8, the hex value is f09f9880, which is 4 bytes. Look at the various representations in the table below:

Format	Value
Emoji	
Code Point	U+1F600
Hexadecimal	f0 9f 98 80
Binary	11110000 10011111 10011000 10000000

Browser	Appl	Goog	FB	Wind	Twtr

You can see here that different places interpret and display the emojis in different ways. It's just like if you have the letter "A," how it appears when it is displayed depends on a variety of factors, like what font you are using.

So, how do computers store emojis? In some senses, it's complicated and has a variety of abstractions and encoding systems. In another sense, it's simple. It's all binary, all 1s and 0s, and there is a method for figuring out how to interpret those 1s and 0s and map them to emojis.

Same Bits, Different Meaning

One of the consequences of different encodings is that the same bits can actually mean totally different things. What's important is to know how to *interpret* the bits.

Say I show you these 8 bits:

`01101011`

What does that mean? Is it a number? Is it a letter? Is it part of a color? There's actually no way to know without more context. It can have meaning as all of those things.

That's the simple and powerful idea of encodings. Once we have the ability to create, store, modify, and share binary data, you can do whatever you want! All you need to do is figure out a way to represent the idea you have in binary. And since sometimes it's a little cumbersome to do it in binary, you can use existing abstractions or encodings that have come before.

So back to our 8-bit string:

`01101011`

What does it mean?

Encoding	Value
Binary	01101011
Decimal	107
Hexadecimal	6B
ASCII	k

So, it doesn't *mean* one particular thing. Also, it is really true that, without the encoding, it doesn't mean anything. It's also possible to interpret some data as one thing when it should be another. What if you are looking at some binary data, and you think it's a color, but it's actually text? There is no reason you can't take the data for an image file and try to open it in a text editor. Actually...try to do that! (On a Mac, try TextEdit. You can drag the file into TextEdit or right-click and select "Open With.") See what happens. You'll see that the text is meaningless. That's because we are interpreting image data as a text file.

Floating-Point Numbers

We've looked at numbers, letters, and images, but what about numbers with decimals? A **floating-point number**, in the simplest version, is a way a computer can represent numbers that have a decimal component. Let's say you want to represent the number 5.18. That's not an integer, so how do you store it? You need a different encoding mechanism.

If you are familiar with scientific notation, you might write the number 3,180 as 3.18 x 10^3.

Where you have an initial number multiplied by 10 raised to a power. This is 3.18 multiplied by 1,000, which is 3,180.

So, if you go into a JavaScript console and type:

```
0.1 + 0.2
```

The answer you get is not 0.3, which is what you'd expect. You actually get:

```
0.30000000000000004
```

Why in the world is that? Shouldn't a computer be able to do something simple like add 0.1 and 0.2? Well, 0.1 and 0.2 aren't integers, so we need to represent the decimal version of them, and this is done as a floating-point number, which is not exact. And so, this simple addition error is actually a result of the way that computers represent floating-point numbers. They are represented by having an initial number (the significand) multiplied by an exponent that is in base-2.

0.1 (base-10) in binary is `0.00011001100110011010`
0.2 (base-10) in binary is `0.0011001100110011011`

If we add those in binary, we get `0.0100110011001101`.

Which is not exactly 0.3; it's a little bit more. This is because we lose precision when converting 0.1 (base-10) to base-2; we only have a limited number of digits in the significand.

There are ways to represent the fraction 1/10 + 2/10, but this is done differently in different programming languages.

True or False: What Are Booleans?

One of the fundamental units for computers is the **boolean**, or a true-or-false value. This is represented both at the hardware and software levels. At the hardware level, it's a transistor. At the software level, it's a true-or-false. More abstractly, a boolean is on or off, or 1 or 0. These all represent the same idea—which is the fundamental idea of a bit, or binary digit. And you can build up all digital information from true/false, 1/0, on/off, and bit. You can see how a bit or a string of bits can represent numbers.

So simply, a boolean value is a true-or-false value.

People to Know

Booleans get their name from George Boole, an English mathematician and philosopher who introduced the idea in his book *The Mathematical Analysis of Logic in 1847.*

Say you want to create a boolean in JavaScript. You could write:

```
var solvedPuzzle = false;
```

Where you are saving the idea of whether or not a user has solved a puzzle. Right now, it is saying that `solvedPuzzle` is `false`, so they have not solved the puzzle. But you could change that to be true:

```
solvedPuzzle = true;
```

This means they did solve the puzzle. In a language like C++, you declare the type of the variable, so you would write:

```
bool solvedPuzzle = false;
```

This says `solvedPuzzle` is a variable that can be `true` or `false`, and currently, it has the value `false`.

Boolean Logic

Booleans are a simple and fundamental unit in computing. A big part of using booleans is finding ways to combine them. **Boolean logic** lets you combine these boolean values, and the starting point is **logical operators**.

The first logical operator to know about is AND, represented in many programming languages with two ampersands (&&). Note: different languages write these operators in different ways. A boolean expression with AND is true if both sides of the expression are true.

```
canVote = over18 and hasRegistered
```

This boolean expression means you can vote in an election if you are over eighteen years old *and* you have registered to vote. If you just did one or the other, then one would be false, and the overall expression would be false. If we wanted to create an expression to see if you could graduate you could write that like this:

```
canGraduate = hasEnoughCredits and
    metRequirements
```

The next logical operator to know about is OR, represented in many programming languages by two vertical bars or pipes (||). For an OR expression to evaluate to **true**, just one side of the expression needs to be true.

```
shouldDrive = lightIsGreen or lightIsYellow
```

Say we are writing the logic of what to do when you approach an intersection. You should keep going if you are at the intersection, and the light is green *or* the light is yellow. Just one of those needs to be **true** to continue.

The next one to know is the NOT operator, represented in many programming languages by the exclamation point (!). Again, there are lots of programming languages, so they represent things in lots of ways.

Here's an example that represents turning on a light switch:

```
lightOn = true;
```

Now, to turn off the light, or "toggle" it between true and false, you can write:

```
lightOn = !lightOn;
```

What that is saying is that `lightOn`, the boolean variable, now gets the new value, which is the opposite of its previous value. So, if it was true before, now it's false.

In our earlier example of approaching an intersection, you might also write:

```
shouldDrive = !lightIsRed
```

This means that `shouldDrive` is `true` if the light is *not* red. Or if the light is red, `shouldDrive` would be `false`, and you should stop.

Truth Tables and Combining Booleans

There's a concept called a **truth table**, which is a table that shows the truth values of the resulting expressions based on a boolean expression. What that means is that if we want to find out what values make a certain boolean expression true or false, we can use this table to fill it in as a way to figure it out.

Here's an example. Say we are doing a truth table for the logical NOT operator.

p	!p
T	F
F	T

What this says is that if we have p being true, then "not p" (or !p, or ¬p in logic notation) is false. And if p is false, then "not p" is true. So, this is a more straightforward one.

Here's what the truth table for AND looks like. An expression is true if both sides of it are true.

p	q	p && q
T	T	T
T	F	F
F	T	F
F	F	F

So, you can see that only the row p = true and q = true leads to p && q being true. Every other combination is false!

Below is the truth table for logical OR.

p	q	p || q
T	T	T
T	F	T
F	T	T
F	F	F

You can see OR is true in three out of four cases. We only need one of p or q to be true.

Now, the more complex truth tables come when you combine these. (There are other logical operators, but we'll stick with these.)

What is the truth table for (x && y) || z? As you can see, they get complicated fast because you need as many rows as $2^{\wedge}$(number of variables). Here, if we have three variables x, y, and z, we need $2^{\wedge}3 = 8$ rows because you need to explore every option if each variable is true or false (2 options (T/F), 3 variables (x, y, z), $2^{\wedge}3 = 8$ total options.

x	y	z	x && y	(x && y) || z
T	T	T	T	T
T	F	T	F	T
F	T	T	F	T
F	F	T	F	T
T	T	F	T	T
T	F	F	F	F
F	T	F	F	F
F	F	F	F	F

Transistors

Transistors are the hardware that enables most of what we know as computers today. It is essentially the switch that represents the "on" or "off," or 1 or 0, on a computer. A memory chip on a computer can have billions of transistors, each storing an "on" or an "off," or a 1 or a 0, and this actually is what stores the information on your computer.

Transistors are made from silicon—which is the reason behind the name for the Silicon Valley area as a technology hub. The transistor was invented in 1947 at Bell Laboratories by John Bardeen, Walter Brattain, and William Shockley, who went on to win the 1956 Nobel Prize in Physics for the invention.

Transistors actually store the 1s and 0s in your computer memory. And the logic of AND, OR, and NOT is built from combining transistors in a circuit. So, this connects your hardware to the logic in your code, or software.

Parts of a Computer

What are the parts that make up a computer? There are many parts, but there are a few that are helpful to know.

You may be familiar with some of the input and output devices. **Input and output**, sometimes called I/O, allows us to connect the computer to the outside world. Input allows us to get information into the system, and output lets us get information back from it. An input device could be a keyboard or a mouse. An output device may be the monitor that shows you graphically what is happening or the sound.

The **storage** is a part of the computer that lets us save data long term. Say you had a photo album with 1,000 family photos, and you want to save those on your computer; those are saved in storage. Your storage might be a **hard drive**, which stores data on a magnetic disk. Or it could be a **solid-state drive**, which stores data in flash memory. If you look at a 2020 MacBook Air, those come with 256GB of storage on a solid-state drive. If the only thing I stored was photos, and each was 3MB, I could store about 85,000 photos.

The **memory** of the computer is where things are stored and accessed for immediate use. When people say "memory," they are often talking about **RAM—Random Access Memory**. Say you were doing math by hand on a scratch paper, and you stored results and intermediate values there; this is like computer memory. The locations in memory are referred to with addresses (usually displayed as hexadecimal values), and you can store binary numbers into locations in memory.

The **CPU**, or **central processing unit**, is the brain of the computer and executes the instructions that make the computer go. It will look at program instructions that it gets from memory and run that instruction. For example, an instruction might be to add two numbers and store the result somewhere in memory. This is like our assembly language or machine code from earlier.

The **motherboard** is the part of the computer that connects the other parts and ensures that they can communicate with each other.

There's more! But those are some of the important pieces.

Year 2038 Bug

With a little bit more background on bits and encodings, you now have the pieces to understand Y2K. The Y2K Bug is like if you tried to store the smiley emoji in the ASCII table—there just wasn't enough space for the data you wanted to store.

We made it through Y2K, but there are new limits from existing data types on the horizon. Now you know that everything on a computer—from a date to a picture to a color to a number to a movie—is represented by digital 1s and 0s. However, the various rules behind the particular encodings can lead to quirky behavior on the edges.

That leads us to the year 2038. Why in the world would that present an issue? In many systems, the way the date is saved is as the number of seconds since January 1, 1970. This is because the time is stored in many systems with Unix time or Epoch time, which is just the number of seconds since 00:00:00 UTC January 1, 1970. This was stored in many places as a 32-bit signed integer. Signed means it can represent positive and negative numbers. Since it is signed, that means the maximum number is $2^{31} - 1$ (31 bits to store the number, and the 32nd bit is representing the sign, positive or negative). So, this number is **2,147,483,647** (in decimal), **7FFF,FFFF** (in hex) and **01111111111111111111111111111111** (in binary).

Number base	Representation of $2^{31} - 1$
10: Decimal	2,147,483,647
16: Hexadecimal	7FFF,FFFF
2: Binary	01111111111111111111111111111111

TRY IT

What Time Is It?

The Unix time as I'm writing this is 1583507183. Can you figure out what the regular date and time are? You can feel free to use Google.

So, at 03:14:08 UTC on Tuesday, January 19, 2038, 2,147,483,647 seconds since the Unix epoch start time, 32-bit versions will stop working. They will then have a problem called **integer overflow**, where when we add 1, instead of getting a number one higher, it will go to a very big negative number and interpret the date as a time in 1901. , with integer overflow, we run out of space to store the number because there aren't enough bits. It's just like what happened with Y2K. There weren't enough numbers to store the full year, so we ran out of space.

What will happen when we get to Y2038? Will we have upgraded the software to avoid this problem? Will it go largely unnoticed? Will people be working diligently behind the scenes to fix this? Only time will tell.

3
How the Internet Works

100101010110100010101010001010100010100101010101010101010110101011001010100101010101010101010110010

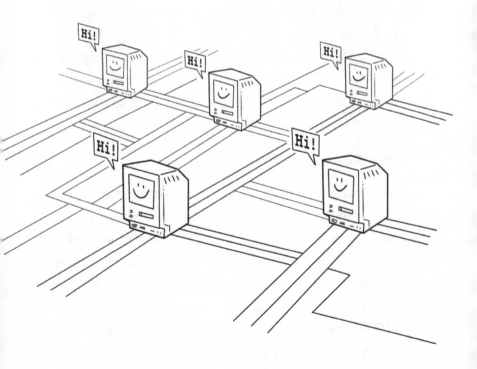

My First Website

I set up my first website, *thekeesh.com*, in 2004. I didn't really have any idea what I was doing, but I purchased a domain and web hosting on *simplehost.com*. "Keesh" was a nickname I had growing up. The first websites I created were simple HTML pages and copy–pasted snippets from different parts of the web. I put up random drawings and inside jokes with friends and used it for a school project. Later, I updated the website to be my blog and a place to host lots of various coding projects I've built. Now, I've been building websites for sixteen years, slowly learning more and getting more advanced. So much of learning about code is just trying it and then experimenting until you get it to work. It's okay if your first site is simple; that is where I started and where everyone needs to start.

How the Internet Works

Understanding how the internet works brings together so many of the things I find fascinating about computing and computer science. There are a few particular topics that fall right at the intersection between the theory and the practice, and how the internet works is one of the topics that exemplifies this best.

This is a topic that has so, so many layers. Even for people who know exactly how so many of these pieces work, there probably isn't anyone who can understand each component at its full level of complexity. So, it's okay if it seems like a lot. Everything along the way is an abstraction built on an abstraction. So, even if someone is an expert in routing, they likely don't also know the nitty-gritty details of how a web browser works and renders pages. What I'll try to do is give an overview of lots of the pieces and show how they fit together to demystify a bit of how the internet works.

So, how does the internet work?

At a high level, the **internet** is a network of networks. It's a network of computers—sometimes your computer, but most of the time, it's other peoples' computers. And using a whole host of technologies, from TCP/IP to DNS to HTTP to routing to JavaScript, you can easily visit a web page just from your computer or phone.

It's a pretty amazing technology. And the more I learn about how it really works, and the more I've uncovered layers of abstraction after trying to demystify this technology now for almost fifteen years, the more it's crazy that it works at all.

The ARPANET

To get a little bit of internet history, when did the internet start? The internet has been building on the history of information and digital technology for hundreds of years. But the first version of today's modern internet was the

ARPANET. **ARPANET** stands for Advanced Research Projects Agency Network and was a project funded out of the Department of Defense. It was set up in 1969.

The first ARPANET message was sent on October 29, 1965 from UCLA to Stanford Research Institute, and the message was "LOGIN." Except that only the first two letters (the L and O) made it through before the system crashed. (Bugs show themselves again.)

The ARPANET was a research project and was only meant for government-related communications. According to a 1982 MIT lab handbook, it was illegal to even use the ARPANET to send personal messages.

In 1969, there were only four nodes on the network: UCLA, Stanford Research Institute, UC Santa Barbara, and the University of Utah.

By 1974, there were still only a few dozen nodes on the ARPANET. Fast forward to 2020, and the modern internet has at least 20 billion nodes.

Web Browsers

We're going to jump around a bit as we explore the internet. We're going to zoom from 1969 on the ARPANET to today in 2020. Today, it's really quite easy to access the internet—from your laptop, from a desktop, from your phone, and even from a wearable, like a watch, or a device, like your thermostat. It's come a long, long way.

So, what is a web browser, and how does that fit into the picture? A **web browser** is the software application you use to access the internet. On my laptop now, I'm using Google Chrome. Other popular web browsers today are Firefox, Safari, Brave, Opera, and Edge. Edge is built by Microsoft, and their previous browser was Internet Explorer.

What can you do on a web browser? Well, at the simplest level, you can type in a URL for a web page, and it will request that web page and show it to you. Now, the question of how it actually does that under the hood is an entirely other story. The web browser sends an **HTTP request**, essentially a way to ask for a website, and receives back HTML. It also may request other files like CSS, images, or JavaScript. (I'll explain all of these things.) The browser then renders all these, interprets them, and figures out what to show you and what to do when you click a button or type a key.

Today, there can actually be a lot of confusion on what a browser is and how the browser differs from the internet. People may assume that Chrome or Safari is the internet—and that isn't right. The browser is the software application that provides an interface to access the internet, but the internet is the actual network. In the 1990s, many people may have thought AOL was the internet; it wasn't.

There are other possible interfaces to access the internet. You could access it by writing a computer program, for example.

> ## People to Know
>
> The first web browser was invented in 1990 by Tim Berners Lee, who is considered the inventor of the World Wide Web. In 1993, Marc Andreessen created the browser Mosaic, and later the company Netscape, which created the Netscape Navigator browser.

Today, Chrome has about 65 percent of the browser market, and Safari has between 15–20 percent. The share of the web browser market has changed quite a bit over time. Internet Explorer had almost the entire market in the early 2000s when it was bundled with the Microsoft Windows operating system.

So, the simplest way to think of the web browser is that it's the program you use to access the internet!

Domain Names

When you open your web browser, you may type in a website like *google.com* or *wikipedia.org*. These are domain names. The **domain name** gives a nice, easy, human-readable way for people to access different sites on the internet. Behind the scenes, there are IP addresses, which are just numbers and a lot harder to remember. Anyone can get a domain name, including you!

I own quite a number of domain names. You can get them for your business or personal website or any other project you want. I have domains at *jeremykeeshin.com* and *thekeesh.com* for my blog, and for work, we have *codehs.com* for CodeHS and *bool.com* for bool.

You can purchase a domain name from a domain name registrar. Today, they cost about $10–$12 per year. The **registrar** is itself a website that helps with the registration and names.

I'd recommend using *misk.com* or *namecheap.com* to get started with buying a domain name. Additionally, there is a part of the domain called the TLD—top-level domain—which is the "extension" or end of the domain name after the dot. So, in *google.com*, the TLD is "com"; in *wikipedia.org*, the TLD is "org."

Recently, there has been an explosion of TLDs as people work to create entire new namespaces. You can purchase a domain on whatever TLD you'd like. Some of the original TLDs were "com," "org," "net," "edu," and "gov." There are now over a thousand TLDs.

URLs

So, what's the difference between a domain name and a URL? What can be tricky about learning about parts of the internet is that lots of words mean very similar things but may be slightly different or have important nuances or distinctions.

A domain name is the basic name that represents your web site, like *codehs.com*. But a URL has more than a domain name—a **URL** is the specific location on the internet. URL stands for Uniform Resource Locator, and it's really just a web address. The domain name is just one part of the URL.

Taking a look at a specific URL, let's look at what the various parts mean: *https://readwritecodebook.com/chapter3*:

- **https** is the **protocol**, saying we are accessing this securely over HTTPS
- *readwritecodebook.com* is the **domain name**, or **hostname**, or website you are visiting
- **com** is the **TLD**, or top-level domain
- **chapter3** is the **path** on the website we are accessing, or the specific location or file we are requesting

A URL is what you'd type into your web browser to get to a specific page or link. The path tells the website exactly which resource you may want to access. Here, we are accessing an HTML page. But a URL could also point to an image or any other resource.

Another important part of a URL is a **subdomain**, which is a part that comes before the domain name. It can be used to organize pages at a high level. Here's an example of how Wikipedia uses subdomains for different language encyclopedias:

URL	Subdomain
en.wikipedia.org	en
en.wikipedia.org	fr

I just accessed the Wikipedia logo at this URL:

*https://upload.wikimedia.org/wikipedia/en/8/80/
Wikipedia-logo-v2.svg*

Here are the various parts:

- **https** is the protocol
- ***wikimedia.org*** is the domain
- **upload** is the subdomain
- ***upload.wikimedia.org*** is the host
- ***/wikipedia/en/8/80/Wikipedia-logo-v2.svg*** is the path
- **org** is the top-level domain

The path, */wikipedia/en/8/80/Wikipedia-logo-v2.svg*, tells it exactly where on the site I want to go. In this case, it will return an image file.

There may be other parts to a URL too! One other more common thing you may see is called the **query**, which is the part after a question mark. This may be used in a search result.

https://www.google.com/search?q=domain

Here the query is "q=domain," which allows a URL to pass a bit more additional information to the web server. This URL is searching Google for the word "domain." Now, as you navigate around the web, take a look at these URLs and see if you can spot some of these different parts.

IP Addresses

We've covered a few pieces that make up the web today so far—the web browser, domain names, and URLs. Now we are going to look one more step behind the scenes to talk about IP addresses. IP stands for Internet Protocol, so an IP address is an Internet Protocol address. But what does that mean?

An **IP address** is a number given to identify devices connected to the internet. An IP address is like a mailing address for a computer on the internet. If you send mail, you need an address, so you know where to go.

An IP address might look something like this:

64.233.160.0

Or this:

66.249.95.255

These are some of the current IP addresses for Google.

When you visit a URL or domain, the domain is just a nicer, easier way to find a computer or device with a particular IP address.

The way most IP addresses are written is in this format, four numbers between 0 and 255 with dots in between. If you remember from earlier, the number 255 and 256 will show up a lot because of bits, bytes, and powers of 2. The numbers 0–255 represent the range of numbers you can create with 8 bits, or 1 byte. IPv4 (which is the format of the IP address here) uses 32 bits, so that is why you have four 8-bit numbers.

It turns out we are actually running out of IPv4 addresses (notice a pattern?), and now there is also a new version, IPv6 with 128 bits, which gives way, way more addresses.

$2^{32} = 4{,}294{,}967{,}296$

$2^{128} = 340{,}282{,}366{,}920{,}938{,}463{,}463{,}374{,}607{,}431{,}\\768{,}211{,}456$

This means there are about 4 billion IPv4 addresses. And 2^{128} is 340 undecillion, so those IPv6 won't run out any time soon.

So, you type in something like *"google.com,"* and that actually translates to an IP address like 66.249.95.255.

Now, the next question you might have is: how exactly do those domain names get translated into IP addresses?

DNS

You may notice there is a lot of lingo and a lot of acronyms that make up the internet. That can make things a bit confusing. Just to review a few of those words before we keep going:

A **domain name** is a string of characters that represents a site on the internet, something like *google.com* or *wikipedia.org*.

A **TLD**, or **top-level domain**, is the extension of the domain name, some of the original common ones being "com," "org," and "edu."

A **URL** is a string of characters that represents a particular resource, location, or page on the internet. It has the protocol and domain name but also the path (and possibly more). For example, *https://en.wikipedia.org/wiki/URL* is a URL pointing to the Wikipedia page about URLs.

An **IP address** is a number that represents an address for a device on the internet. It's the address in a form that's easier for a computer to read. An IP address looks like this: 209.85.128.0.

Okay, now, with these helpful ideas, the next thing to understand is DNS. So, what is DNS? **DNS** stands for the Domain Name System. One of the key functions is to translate domain names to IP addresses, exactly the thing we were wondering about earlier!

You type in *google.com*, and then it tells you to go find the computer with IP address 66.249.95.255. That's what DNS does. Now, the question is: how exactly does it do that?

Say we have a domain like:

en.wikipedia.org

The way we get to the IP address is, first, by starting all the way on the right, with the TLD. So, in this example, the TLD, or domain extension, is "org." There is a starting point for DNS, which is the root zone, and then there are places to go next to find "org." And then from "org," we go one name to the left to see where to go to find Wikipedia.

What happens is: from the DNS system, you can get to certain DNS records that tell you, "Okay, you wanted to get to *en.wikpedia.org*; to do that, you should go to this IP address!" There are more steps in between, but essentially DNS is the system for mapping names that are easier for people to read, to IP addresses which are easier for computers to understand.

HTTP

The start of many of our URLs is http:// or https://—what does that part mean? That is the protocol. HTTP stands for HyperText Transfer Protocol. **HTTP** is the protocol for actually making requests from websites. So, the client, or user, makes a request in HTTP, and the server provides a response.

The request is something like:

```
GET /
Host: www.google.com
```

This is saying, "Can I get the web page for *www.google. com?*"

The server then sends a response. So, HTTP is the way that clients and servers communicate with each other. There are different types of methods for HTTP, some of the main ones being GET (to get a web page) and POST (to save data).

You may get a response with a status code like **200**, which means it is all working.

But you also may get a status code like **404**, meaning that page doesn't exist. And **500**, meaning there was a server error. Have you ever seen a cryptic error like **404** or **500** on a website? Now, you know what it means: it's a type of HTTP status code for a request that didn't complete successfully.

To test this out, here is how you could request the HTTP response headers from my blog. If you have a Mac, open the Terminal application and type:

```
curl -I https://thekeesh.com
```

Here was the HTTP response I got; 200 means it went through successfully:

```
HTTP/1.1 200 OK
Date: Tue, 05 May 2020 14:27:35 GMT
Server: Apache/2.4.29 (Ubuntu)
Vary: Accept-Encoding,Cookie
Cache-Control: max-age=3, must-revalidate
Content-Length: 53895
Last-Modified: Tue, 05 May 2020 14:17:44 GMT
Content-Type: text/html; charset=UTF-8
```

When it starts with HTTPS, this means it is using an encrypted connection.

TCP/IP

Okay, now we need to go one layer down to continue to understand how the internet works. When you send a message across the internet, the way it's really working is it's being broken up into parts, or packets, which are then reassembled on the other side. Say you have your message, request, or file; it's actually split up and sent across the network, but it can take various paths. On the way back, the pieces may have been jumbled and need to be reassembled for it to make sense. This is what the TCP (Transmission Control Protocol) is doing.

With TCP, it's like sending the pieces of a puzzle, but the puzzle pieces may come out of order. **TCP** ensures the puzzle pieces are assembled correctly. It's like if you had some letter written on paper and were going to send it in the mail, but you took the letter, cut it up into pieces, put each piece in its own envelope, numbered them one to ten, and mailed them separately. Each piece may take a different route, but at the end, TCP will make sure all ten pieces got there and will order them and tape them together. TCP is guaranteeing the delivery of the full message.

TCP/IP are often referred to together. The IP is lower level and is focused on the address of the destination. The IP component is just responsible for delivering the slices of the message, the packets, and is not always fully reliable. But the TCP layer is the reliable layer and is built upon the IP layer.

In the diagram, you can see an overview of the internet model with four layers, and each layer is built upon the next. HTTP as a protocol is built upon TCP, which is built upon IP, which is built upon the network layer like Ethernet or Wi-Fi.

Network Layer	Sample Protocol
Application	HTTP
Transport	TCP
Internet	IP
Link	Ethernet

People to Know

The TCP/IP protocols were created by Robert Kahn and Vinton Cerf, who are considered the creators of the internet. Their publication of the TCP protocol in 1974 was the first known use of the word "internet," which was shorthand for internetwork. (TCP is an inter-network communication protocol.)

HTML

So, we've looked a bit at browsers, domain names, and protocols, but when you get to the actual website, how does someone actually code that up? The answer is: using HTML. There are other parts as well, but at the most basic level, **HTML** is what is used to create the structure of websites. HTML stands for HyperText Markup Language. When you make an HTTP request, the server will often give you back HTML.

HTML is made up of tags, something like `<p>` or `<div>`. These tags essentially show how you want the page to look. Here's a sample of a complete tag, called an `<h1>` tag, which makes a large header on a page.

```
<h1>My First Website</h1>
```

Tags start with an opening tag and end with a closing tag, where the closing tag has the extra "/" character.

My First Website

This is what that will look like when actually rendered. The tags don't show up. If you go and use the trick from earlier, where you right-click on a website and select "View Page Source," what you are seeing is the HTML.

You can see what the code creates for anything in this chapter by looking at the examples on *readwritecodebook. com.*

There are many different types of tags. There are tags for headers and paragraphs, different sections of the page, lists, and navigation bars. At a high level, the tags are for different structural elements. The tags are hierarchical, where tags can be inside other tags. A way to think about it is like an outline.

If you are making an outline, you may have something like:

1. Topic 1
   a. Subtopic
   b. Another point
2. Topic 2
   a. Argument 1
   b. Argument 2
   c. Argument 3
      i. Piece of evidence

This outline structure is related to HTML tags. Argument 1 here is nested under Topic 2. In HTML, you may have a section within a section or a paragraph within a certain division of the page.

CSS

HTML is responsible for the structure of the page. But if you load a page and everything seems to look all wrong or just looks plain, then you may have been loading an HTML page without the CSS. The HTML outlines the structure, but the **CSS** determines the style and design of the page.

CSS stands for Cascading Style Sheets. Essentially, with CSS, you can choose an HTML element, or a specific set of tags or related elements, and say how you want to style them. When you say how you want to style them, you can change the font, the color, the size, the margins (the spacing around the elements), and many more things.

For example, if you wanted to say that all text within paragraphs should be red, you'd write a CSS rule like this:

```
p {
   color: red;
}
```

A CSS rule shows which elements you want to select and then what things to style about them. So, when you say `color: red`, you are setting the "color" property to have the value "red."

JavaScript

There are whole books and courses on HTML, CSS, and JavaScript, but the idea here is to help you get a sense of where these all fit in as part of the larger web and as part of the body of knowledge around computer science. If any topic here interests you, I hope you dive in more!

When you talk about creating websites, you've now seen how HTML sets the structure of the page, and CSS sets the design and style of the page. JavaScript is responsible for the interactivity and logic on the page. How does something respond when you click? Or how do you create an animation? Or how do you make something as complicated as Twitter or Google Docs? Those websites all involve JavaScript.

JavaScript is a programming language that is also considered a scripting language. If you want to try running JavaScript right in the web browser, right-click and open up the console. Right-click, select "Inspect," and then click "Console."

Try typing:

```
2 + 2
```

Then enter. That's evaluating a JavaScript expression—it works a little bit like a calculator with a few special rules.

Try typing:

```
console.log("Hello");
```

That will print "Hello" out to the console like "Hello World" from earlier.

And if you want to create a popup, try writing:

```
alert("Hey!")
```

There's a lot, lot more to JavaScript, but this gives you an idea of what it is and where it fits in.

Take a look at JavaScript running on a web page at the examples on *readwritecodebook.com*.

Blogs

You may have heard of a blog. What's a blog, and how can you get one? Well, the word **blog** is short for "web log." There are now lots of ways to get started with either reading blogs or creating your own blog. If you've browsed the internet, you've probably stumbled upon a blog. A blog is just a place to write articles, or blog posts. Individuals can have blogs; companies and other organizations can have blogs; even other types of publications may format their content as a blog. What's the line between a blog and another form of publishing? Well, it's not a hard and fast line. *The New York Times* has many blogs. Blog content may often be more short-form (but it doesn't have to be!) or more real-time (but it also doesn't have to be!)—but there are many, many types of blogs out there.

If you want to create your own blog, here are a few ways you can do that: You can create a blog that someone else hosts on a site like Medium or Blogger. You can also host your own blog—meaning the content lives on your own web server. A common blog platform is WordPress, which can be used in a way that is hosted on WordPress or on your own site. The code is all open source, meaning it's available and accessible for you to use and install. I have a handful of blogs, some that are hosted and some that I host on my own servers. For the self-hosted blogs, I use normally use WordPress.

View Source

One goal here is to demystify a bit about how coding and the internet works. When you visit a URL, it sends you some code to run in your web browser, including HTML, CSS, and JavaScript. It turns out you have access to view all that code! If you right-click on any website, and in the dropdown, select "View Source" or "View Page Source," it will show you the code that is creating that web page. Here, when the word "source" is used, it is referring to the code, similar to the phrase "source code." So, you could use "source code," "source," or "code" almost interchangeably.

If you view the source, what you will see is the HTML that creates the page. Then, there may also be links to other resources, like CSS and JavaScript, which control the design, logic, and interactivity on the page.

You'll see in some sites you can parse out a bit of what is going on. In others, it will just look like random letters. A big reason for this is the code is often compressed before it is sent to you and also obfuscated, which means intentionally made smaller to save space and harder to read.

Because the web is built on open technologies, "View Source" is something I've used throughout a long time of exploring the internet to understand how it works.

TRY IT

View Source

Try visiting a website and clicking "View Source"! Try it on a few different sites. Right-click on any website, and in the dropdown, select "View Source" or "View Page Source." (On a Mac, I can also use the shortcut option + command + U.)

Going to the Console

This is a part of the web browser that I suspect most people don't know about that lets you explore a little bit more under the hood. If you right-click again (right-click seems to be the first step to unlocking the underworld of coding) and click "Inspect" (usually next to "View Source"), it will pop open a section in your browser. What it pops open is the developer **console** and, usually, a bunch of tools to actually help in the building and debugging of websites.

Here, I'll write a bit about how specifically the Chrome developer console works. You'll see tabs for Elements, Console, Network, and several more.

If you visit *The New York Times*, for example, right-click on a headline, and select "Inspect," it will open up the Elements tab of the developer console with the particular HTML that is creating the headline that is highlighted! It's actually really cool to see.

What you'll see is a `<span>` tag or `<a>` tag, which is an **anchor**, or **link tag**. It means, when you click on that, it goes to another web page. If you now double-click on the actual text of the headline within the console, it will become an editable text box. And once it's editable, you can type in your own headline, like "Great Book Shows You How to Change Headlines." If you do that and click enter, you'll see your headline looks like it is in *The New York Times*!

The web has really always been about remixing, and the easy ability to view, copy, and remix source code in HTML, CSS, and JavaScript is a way to both learn and explore web design.

Now, if you go to the Console tab, you may see different messages depending on what website you are visiting. Here is a console where you can run JavaScript. Try typing 2 + 2, then enter. You'll see 4 printed out. You can write any JavaScript here or use it to explore web pages. There are lots of accessible functions to explore the web page as well. If you start by typing `document`, you'll see lots of possible things to type appear. While you are there, try clicking around the other tabs to see what they do. The Network tab will actually show you the web requests being made by the browser. With the Network tab open, try to refresh the page to see what happens.

Getting Your Own Domain Name

You can get your own web page on the internet in lots of different ways now. But a big step towards diving a bit more under the hood is getting your own domain name. This is a domain name like *google.com*, *wikipedia.org*, *thekeesh.com*, and *jeremykeeshin.com*. Once you have this name, you have your own little virtual plot of cyberspace. You can then go point the DNS records and address wherever you want. You could point it at your own computer, or you could point it at your own web hosting service, your own web server, or even another site that helps you make websites. There are lots of options.

There are a couple of steps to getting your own domain name. The first is checking that the domain you want is available. If it's available, then great! Continue on to purchase it. If it's not, you can try to come up with another domain name. Or you can look into different domain extensions. The most common extensions are .com and .org, but certain websites and startups (as well as domain name registrars), have popularized or attempted to popularize other extensions like .io, .ly, .co, .me...and a lot of others. An easy place to start is on a website like *instant domainsearch.com*, which allows you to easily search for available domain names.

Then you'll want to go to a domain name registrar to buy your domain. Most .com domains will cost about $10–$12 per year. Some of the newer extensions will have a higher premium price (You're not getting anything different; it's just a different domain.)

I've used lots and lots of domain name registrars. Now, the ones I use most often that I recommend are:

- Namecheap: *namecheap.com*
- Misk: *misk.com*
- Google Domains: *domains.google*

I specifically do not recommend GoDaddy and highly recommend that you avoid it. This has been a very scammy site with poor business practices and often upsells unsuspecting or less tech-savvy customers add-ons that don't do much or simply aren't needed. When you want a domain name, just get the name.

Then, you can search for the domain on your registrar of choice, create an account, and purchase the domain. You'll usually purchase a domain for a year, but if you want, you can purchase for multiple years. You'll be asked to enter in certain contact information, which is listed in the WHOIS database—a public record of domain contact information. Remember, this is public, so it's easily available. Some registrars offer to keep your contact information private or do that for a fee.

Now you have your domain name! You can now point it where you want by setting the nameservers. Sometimes this takes one to two hours or up to a day or two to propagate these changes through the internet.

Getting Your Own Web Hosting or Server

Once you have your own domain name, you will want to actually have your website show something. You'll need a place for those files or code to exist. It could be your own computer. But your computer might not always be on, or easily redundant. So, there are lots of companies that exist that provide web hosting, or the ability to host your code for your website. You could also get a web server, which in many cases is more complete access to a computer or part of a computer that someone else is managing.

When I made my first websites, I had some random web hosting site. It's actually, in some ways, a nice way to start because it doesn't expose all the complexity of starting with your own server, which is what I have now. For CodeHS—and for many websites—instead of just one server, we have many different servers.

If you want web hosting, this comes in lots of different flavors. At a high level, with web hosting, you are getting a place to put your HTML, CSS, and JavaScript files and possibly other server code. It's basically like a folder that represents the files on your website. I'm generally not a fan of web hosting companies, and a lot of the cheaper ones sell deceptive pricing plans that seem really cheap but lock you into a term longer than you may want. A sample web hosting site would be a site like HostGator, BlueHost, or NearlyFreeSpeech.NET. Buying web hosting is a simpler way to start.

If you get access to a server, you'll usually be buying access to some computer resources for a certain period of time or paying for the time and computer resources you use. A few ways you can get started with getting a server—these are all sites I have used—are DigitalOcean, Linode, or AWS (Amazon Web Services). Setting up a web server on these sites is much more complicated than setting up web hosting. As of today, on DigitalOcean, you can get a server for $5 per month, so it is cheap to get started. You can do quite a lot on all these by getting a server for around $20–$40 per month. I host many, many websites on a single virtual server.

Steps for Setting Up Web Hosting

Here is a specific process to get your own website on the internet with your own web hosting. At CodeHS, we also have an easy way to create your own home, where you can write HTML, CSS, and JavaScript and get a custom *codehs.me* subdomain. (Mine is at *jkeesh.codehs.me*.)

Step 1: Register Web Hosting Account

Go to *nearlyfreespeech.net* and sign up. They offer web hosting starting at 1¢ per day, and you can try it for free. Once your profile is created, create an account. Once your account is created, create a site. You'll enter in your unique site name. I also suggest you go and change your password.

Step 2: Buy the Domain

Pick the name of your website. I bought the domain *setupyourwebhosting.com* on *nearlyfreespeech.net* for $10 per year. This is a real website with these instructions. You can buy the domain under the Domains tab and then click "Register a New Domain." When prompted about DNS, choose "Set up DNS and Name Servers Automatically."

Step 3: Download an FTP Program

The FTP program will allow you to upload files onto your site. FTP stands for File Transfer Protocol. Download Cyberduck and install it.

Step 4: Set Up a Text Editor

I downloaded Sublime Text to write code on my computer.

Step 5: Create an `index.html` File

We're going to create the file that will show up on your website. Open Sublime Text. Create a new file. In that file, just type:

```
<h1>Welcome to my first website!</h1>
```

Then save that file on your Desktop as `index.html`. Now double-click that file. It will open in your web browser, and it should look like this:

My First Website

Step 6: Upload Your HTML File to Your Site with FTP

Now go to *nearlyfreespeech.net* and open the "Sites" tab. Click into the site you created. There should be a section that shows your SSH/SFTP information.

Open Cyberduck. Click "+" to create a connection.

Under "Server," enter your SSH/SFTP Hostname. Under "Username" and "Password," enter your username from the SSH/SFTP section and your password for the site. Once you are connected, you will be in a folder with nothing in it. Now drag your `index.html` file from your Desktop into this folder in Cyberduck.

When it's uploaded, you will see the `index.html` file appearing in Cyberduck.

Step 7: Connect Your Domain to Your Site

Click into your site under the "Sites" tab. Under "Site Names & Aliases," click "Add a New Alias." Now enter in the name you just bought. I typed in *www.setupyourweb hosting.com*. Then, I also went and added *setupyourweb hosting.com* as another alias.

Step 8: Visit your site!

It should work! Visit your website now and you should see your site load with the text you typed in `index.html`. You can also revisit these instructions at *setupyourweb hosting.com*.

Configuring the Website for This Book

Take, for example, the website for this book (*readwrite-codebook.com*). How exactly did I set that up? This is the advanced way that shows the full set of steps.

Step 1: Buy the Domain

I bought the domain *readwritecodebook.com* on Google Domains (*https://domains.google/*), which is $12 per year.

Step 2: Point the Nameservers to My Linode Account

I clicked into the DNS tab on Google Domains and selected "Use custom name servers" since I was configuring my

name servers on Linode. I pointed this domain to the
Linode nameservers:

```
ns1.linode.com
ns2.linode.com
ns3.linode.com
ns4.linode.com
ns5.linode.com
```

This means that when you go to this domain and ask,
"What IP address do I go to?" it asks the nameservers here
to give us that information.

**Step 3: Set My A-Records to Point
to My Server IP Address in Linode**

On my Linode account, I set up a new domain, and I
had the A-records set up to point to my web server IP
address. My web server IP address is 173.230.152.171.
An A-record maps from a domain to an IP address. This
says going to *readwritecodebook.com* will go to this IP
address.

**Step 4: Configure the Virtual Server
to Go to the Right Folder**

Next, I made a folder on my web server for the website
called *readwritecodebook.com* and added an HTML file to
it. I started with a file called `index.html`.

Then, I created a configuration file for the web server to know where to go for this domain. This part is all more advanced.

Step 5: That's it.

Visit *readwritecodebook.com* to test the website. Now, the last few steps can be tricky, but this shows you how you connect from the domain to the nameservers to the IP address to the virtual server to the actual files. I've created maybe fifty sites, so I'm familiar with this process, but I'd recommend starting with a domain name and web hosting. Just getting your own domain up with your own HTML file (that you coded!) is quite an accomplishment. That was how I started. You can use lots of website builders today that abstract away that whole thing, but this is how you go under the hood.

Clients and Servers

The language of clients and servers is essential to understanding the internet. Lots of the things we have already discussed can be understood better in the language of clients and servers. The **client** is whoever or whatever is using the service, and the **server** is what is providing the service. Another way to think about it is that when you are the client, you are the user of some particular website. And the server is the computers controlled by the website.

So, the client is really your computer. And the server is someone else's computer.

When you visit a website, you are making a **request** to that website, which will be handled by the server. Here's what it looks like for our client to make an HTTP request for a website from a server for Google and receive back HTML. Now you understand all the pieces!

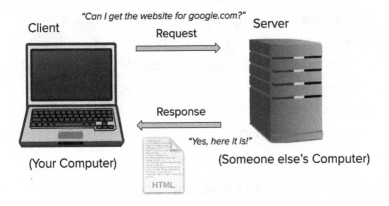

Now that there is a basic understanding here of client and server, we can start to see how this fits into other things.

The client is the end user and is usually your computer.

The server is the provider of the website and is usually someone else's computer.

The client, what you use, really is just the **front end** of the website.

The server can also be thought of as the behind-the-scenes component, or the **back end** of the website.

Now, there are programmers who work on the front end or back end. The front end deals with the client-facing part—or what you see. That's the HTML, CSS, and JavaScript! That's everything that actually gets sent to your computer and browser and rendered. That's the client side or the front end.

The back end for the web is much more varied. There are some languages that can be used as back-end languages, like Python, Ruby, Java, JavaScript, or many, many others.

But the key idea here to know in the client/server model of the web is there is one party who requests things (usually you, the end user), and the server provides a response (from their computer).

Issues to Know: Net Neutrality and Censorship

What is net neutrality, and why should you care? There are so many topics that animate the future discourse of the web, and net neutrality is a crucial one. At this point, you have the pieces to understand what the debate is about. **Net neutrality** concerns whether all the bits being transferred on the web are considered equal or if some can be prioritized.

Part of what this means is that there is a level playing field for all websites at the infrastructure level, from a tiny blog to a massive tech company. The issue if there isn't net neutrality is that it quickly becomes unfair. This would allow your ISP, or internet service provider (like Comcast, AT&T, or Charter), to pick winners. They could unfairly slow or speed up certain websites or offer companies priority access if they pay more. Taken to the extreme, the ISP could inspect the websites you are visiting and decide to block them or slow them down at their own discretion.

This is a key issue related to internet access, censorship, and, really, the functioning of the decentralized web. The US currently does not have net neutrality. In China, there are many restrictions on the web known as the "Great Firewall." This means the government controls what sites people can access and can fully block businesses from operating. Major US websites are blocked in China, including Google, YouTube, Facebook, and Wikipedia. This is all against net neutrality, and from my perspective, you'll continue to see net neutrality and censorship as key issues for the future of the internet.

4
Programming Concepts

100101010101010100101010100001010100101001010101010101010111101010110010101010010101010101001010101010010101

One time I was on *The Today Show* for about a minute, holding a stuffed-animal dog, being interviewed by Al Roker. It makes slightly more sense when you understand why. We had been competing in an *NBC* challenge called the Education Nation Innovation Challenge and won a prize, so we had a short interview. Our mascot at CodeHS is Karel the Dog, a friendly dog to help learn programming. So, of course, I brought Karel when we were on the show. Coding can be intimidating, and starting in a friendly way makes it more accessible.

No one just knows computer science concepts intrinsically. You learn them and practice them like any skill. Although the jargon of coding can be intimidating, when we teach it, we try to make it as friendly as possible to begin, and that's why we use Karel the Dog.

To actually control the computer or tell it what to do, you need to program it or code it. You'll start with the idea in your head of the program—or the app, the website, the function, or whatever it is you want to make—and you have to figure out how to translate it into a language that the computer can understand.

And the language that the computer can understand is very specific—it's a code. It has rules for syntax, and it's not nearly as flexible as talking to another person, who can maybe figure out what you mean.

Karel the Dog

At CodeHS, we start teaching programming with Karel the Dog, and I've used Karel to help teach basic coding to kids and adults. **Karel** is a friendly dog who lives in a grid world. We can solve different puzzles or problems by writing code for Karel. There will always be a starting position for Karel and the world and then an ending position. Karel can move around the world and put down and take tennis balls. By just using this as a building block, we can introduce coding and explain the main concepts.

Karel was created as an educational programming language by Richard Pattis and is based on the name Karel Čapek, a writer who introduced the word "robot." I learned about Karel, and we taught intro courses with a version of Karel at Stanford. Here is a picture of Karel the Dog.

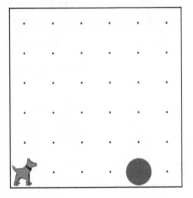

Commands

Writing code is giving instructions or giving **commands** to a computer, just like giving commands to a dog. Actually, the computer will follow your instructions a lot more carefully than your real-life dog will—Karel is luckily a computerized dog, so that makes it a bit easier.

Karel knows just four commands, and those commands are:

```
move();
turnLeft();
putBall();
takeBall();
```

That's it. Just four. The move(); command moves Karel one spot forward in the direction they are facing. The turnLeft(); command rotates Karel 90 degrees to the left, so for example, if Karel is facing east, and you write turnLeft();, now Karel will be facing north.

Here is our first program with one command.

Program: First Program

```
move();
```

Left: starting world. Right: after Karel runs the move(); command.

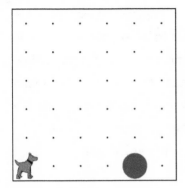 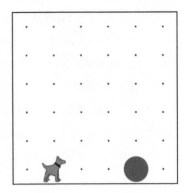

Program: Second Program

```
move();
turnLeft();
```

Left: starting world. Right: after Karel runs the move();
and turnLeft(); commands.

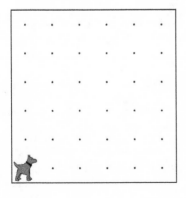 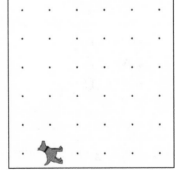

A command is almost like a regular word, but there are a few specific rules. First, it has to be exactly one of those four words with no spaces and the same capitalization; that's all that Karel understands. Right now, we are using Karel's language, but behind the scenes, we are using the JavaScript programming language.

Next, each command has to end with:

```
();
```

This is how the computer actually understands that it is a command, and this is the syntax for calling a command in the language. And that is it.

So, say we want to write a program that moves Karel twice and puts down a ball. Our program then looks like this.

Program: Third Program

```
move();
move();
putBall();
```

Left: starting world. Right: ending world after the code has run.

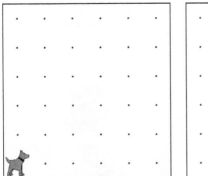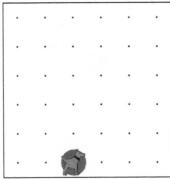

That's it! Karel then goes one by one through the commands. Say you want to write your own program. How could you write code to get Karel to move four times and then take the ball on that spot? Here is the starting and ending world:

Program: Write a Karel Program

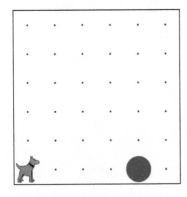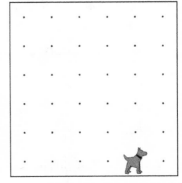

Say you want to write code to have Karel build a pyramid like the grid below; what would the commands be?

Program: Pyramid Karel

 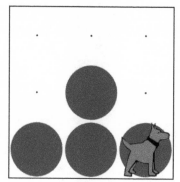

TRY IT

Write Your First Karel Program

Now that you've seen the Karel commands, try to run these programs. You can try running and writing any of these programs in the examples for this chapter at *readwritecodebook.com*.

Functions

The first programming concept to understand is commands. Commands are the instructions you can give to a computer or to Karel and are the most basic building blocks. But once you keep playing around with Karel, you run into some limitations. You only get four commands. But what if you need more? Right now, Karel is pretty limited and can't even turn right.

How might you get Karel to turn right just with the set of commands that you have? Only one command can even change the direction of Karel, and that is the turnLeft(); command. So, if you want to turn right, can you think of a way?

(Try to think of this on your own for a minute.)

To get Karel to turn right, you can actually turn left three times. Three lefts get us facing the same direction as turning right.

That might look like this:

```
turnLeft();
turnLeft();
turnLeft();
```

So, now, at least you have a workaround when you need to turn right. You can write turnLeft(); three times instead. But as your programs get more complex and challenging, this gets to be a bit of a hassle and not very clear. You'd like to be able to just tell Karel to turn right.

This is where functions come in. **Functions** let you teach Karel a new word or new command. You give the new command a name, and then you write the list of commands you want to happen when you run this new command.

Creating this new **command** is called defining a function, and if we wanted to define the `turnRight()` function to have Karel turn left three times, it would look like this:

```
function turnRight()
{
  turnLeft();
  turnLeft();
  turnLeft();
}
```

This is the **syntax**, or rules for creating a new function. We use the word function, then our new name, then ( ). Then, between a pair of open and close curly brackets ({ and }, putting them one on each line to start off), we write the list of commands we want to happen. That's it; that is how you define a function.

Then when you want Karel to actually do the command, you call the function. The way to call a function is like this:

```
turnRight();
```

So, **calling a function** is just like giving a command; that's because we've created a new command.

Let's create one more function. Say you wanted Karel to turn around. To turn around, Karel would need to turn left

Write a Function

Now that we have a few handy functions, how might you create your own? Say you wanted to create a function to move Karel twice called `moveTwice()`, how would you code that? Say you wanted to write a function to move Karel up one spot called `moveUp()`, how would you code that? As an additional challenge, how could you write a `buildBox()` function to create a square of tennis balls and call it three times? You can try these challenges at *readwritecodebook.com*.

twice. So, that function would look like this. Let's define the function:

```
function turnAround()
{
  turnLeft();
  turnLeft();
}
```

Now, if we wanted to call the function, it would look like this:

```
turnAround();
```

Loops

Now you've been introduced to Karel: our friendly dog that helps us learn programming and understands a very specific language. Giving commands to a computer, or coding, is just like giving commands to a dog. Once we have commands, we can build those up to create our own new commands, or functions. Functions give us a way to make something easier to understand and repeatable, and to create new building blocks.

But say the problems got a bit more challenging. Now the grid is a lot bigger. The grid is now 20x20. Or even 100x100. And say you want to have Karel move around the grid and put down a ball in every location. You could go and write out the commands, but that is a lot of typing. It would just take too long and be too repetitive. What do you do when you need to repeat things? Karel has an answer for that.

When we want to repeat things in our code, we can use loops. There are two main types of loops to know: `for` loops and `while` loops.

For loops let us repeat code a fixed number of times.

While loops let us repeat code while some condition is true.

So, to look at an example: say you wanted Karel to move 57 times—you would use a for loop because that is a specific number of times. Here's the code for that:

```
for(var i = 0; i < 57; i++)
{
    move();
}
```

There is a lot of syntax here, but what it does is say, "Repeat the move(); command times." All you do is change the number 57 to however many times you want it to happen. So, if you wanted Karel to move 8 times instead, you would write:

```
for(var i = 0; i < 8; i++)
{
    move();
}
```

Now, within the for loop, you can write any block of code, you can write a command, many commands, or call functions. Here would be code to have Karel move and put down a ball 10 times.

```
for(var i = 0; i < 10; i++)
{
  move();
  putBall();
}
```

The next type of loop is a while loop. A while loop lets us repeat code as long as some condition is true. Why might we need while loops? Say we want to repeat something, but we don't know the specific number of times in advance, we would use a while loop.

With Karel, say we wanted to move to the end of a row. If there was just one grid we were solving for, we would be fine with a for loop. We could count the number of times to move to get us to the other end and write a for loop for that. But what if there are many grids? What if we wanted to write one program to get Karel to the other end of the world, but we don't know if the world is 10 spaces, 20 spaces, or 100 spaces wide? Then, we'd use a while loop.

One other thing Karel can do is ask certain questions about the world, or conditions.

For example, Karel can find out if the front is clear to move. The code for that is:

```
frontIsClear()
```

The answer here is either true—yes, the front is clear—or

false—no, the front is not clear. This condition returns a boolean value.

Say we want to write the code to move Karel to the end of the row. Say the starting world and ending world look like the 6x6 world in the Move to Wall program example, but now we have to make it work for different types of worlds.

Program: Move to Wall

6x6 World

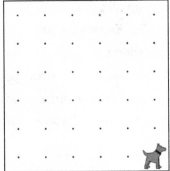

10x10 World

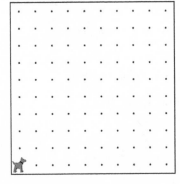
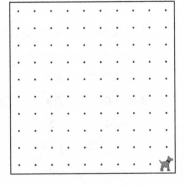

The code would be:

```
while(frontIsClear())
{
   move();
}
```

What happens in a while loop is Karel asks the question at the top: "Is the front clear?" If the answer is yes, then we run all the code in between the curly brackets ({ and }). So, Karel will ask, "Is the front clear?" Then move. And then ask again: "Is the front clear?" Then move. And keep doing that. At some point, Karel will ask: "Is the front clear?" and the answer will be no. The program will be over, and we will have reached the other side of the world.

TRY IT
Loops

Try running the programs from this section at *readwritecodebook.com*. Now try to modify the number in the for loop to have Karel change the number of times they repeat the loop.

So, those are the two types of loops: `for` loops, for when we want to repeat code a fixed number of times, and `while` loops, for when we want to repeat code as long as some condition is true.

Conditionals

Now we have a few of the building blocks with Karel.

You have **commands**: the basic building block, an instruction that Karel can do.

You have **functions**: these let you teach Karel a new trick or create a new command out of a list of other existing instructions.

You have **loops**: these let Karel repeat a block of code. `For` loops let us repeat code a fixed number of times, and `while` loops let us repeat code while some condition is true.

You have **conditions**: these let Karel ask questions about the world.

There are a few different ways you can use conditions. The idea of a conditional statement is that certain code will run only if some condition is true.

Earlier, we saw that Karel can check certain questions about the world, like asking if the front is clear.

Here are a few other things Karel can check:

```
frontIsClear()
frontIsBlocked()
ballsPresent()
noBallsPresent()
facingNorth()
facingSouth()
facingEast()
facingWest()
```

Each of these is a condition, or question Karel can ask about the world. For example, say we want to take a ball from the current spot; we need to ensure there is a ball there, or if we try to take a ball, we will run into an error.

So, what conditional statements do is let us run code only if a condition is true. There are a few formats.

First is the **if** statement.

The **if** statement looks like this:

```
if(CONDITION)
{
    CODE
}
```

So, we only run the code block if the condition is true. CONDITION would be filled in by any of the questions Karel can ask. For example:

```
if(ballsPresent())
{
   takeBall();
}
```

The next version we have is the `if/else` statement. The `if/else` statement lets us do one thing if a condition is true, and something else if the condition is not true. Say we wanted to take a ball if it is there, and if it is not there, put a ball. The code for that would be:

```
if(ballsPresent())
{
   takeBall();
}
else
{
   putBall();
}
```

You can also check various conditions in a row by writing an `else-if` statement, which lets you check conditions one by one and then have a catch-all if needed. That looks like this:

```
if(CONDITION)
{
   CODE
}
else if(CONDITION)
{
   CODE
}
else
{
   CODE
}
```

Control Flow

Loops and conditional statements are control structures that define the order of instructions. In a program with just commands, Karel will start at the top and go one by one, doing the commands in order as written. However, the **control flow**, which is the order that instructions happen in, can be altered by control structures. Instead of just continuing to go one by one, a `for` loop or `while` loop lets us repeat a certain block of code.

If we have an if statement or an `if/else` statement, then the program won't just go line by line—it may jump around depending on the result of those questions.

With the control structures in Karel, loops and conditionals, the way it works is this: Karel has to ask a question of some sort, and then, depending on the result, different things could happen.

In a `for` loop, we ask the question, "Have we repeated this the right number of times?" The yes/no answer there lets us know what to do next.

In a `while` loop, we ask the question, "Is this condition true?" The yes/no answer lets us know what to do next.

In an `if` statement or `if/else` statement, we ask the question, "Is the condition true?" Then, we run the corresponding block of code.

Top-Down Design

One of the best ways to learn coding is to just try it out, and there will be ideas in the book that you can try out along the way. Now that you have the basics—you know commands, functions, loops, and conditionals—how can you put them together to write a more complicated program?

Say you wanted to have Karel write a program to build three flags of tennis balls. How might you do that? One option is to go code all the individual commands one at a time. But then your program is hard to read and understand.

The better way to do this is to start with the program that you want and break it down into smaller problems.

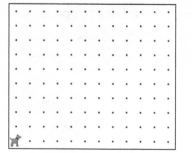 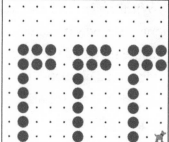

Say we started in the world on the left and wanted to end up in the world on the right, where Karel has built three flags. Here, we will imagine that we already had functions that we can use. We are just going to assume that we have a function called `buildFlag()` that has Karel build a flag. The idea is first we try to describe in English what we want to do at a high level. This is called **pseudocode**. If we had that `buildFlag()` function, our program would be very easy. I'll also assume we have a function to move to the next flag. Initially, in top-down design, we outline the overall plan for the program and don't yet worry about the details.

So, the pseudocode for my program might be like:

```
move
build flag
move to next flag
build flag
move to next flag
build flag
```

This is a clear English description of the steps we want to take. Now, each line I've written becomes its own function call. It's okay if a function doesn't exist—we'll write it later.

So, now my code would look like this:

```
move();
buildFlag();
moveToNextFlag();
buildFlag();
moveToNextFlag();
buildFlag();
```

Now it's starting to look like code. But we don't have the buildFlag() function! So, the next thing to do is write it. We can write each function first as pseudocode and then in code.

Let's write buildFlag().

```
// Assume we start on the position we want
// to build a flag, on the bottom row
// Assume we end on the bottom row after we
// have built the flag in the rightmost
// position
function buildFlag
   buildPole
   buildRectangle
   comeDown
```

My strategy here is to build the pole, which is the bottom five balls, then to build a rectangle, which is a 3x2 rectangle. Then, we would come down to the first row.

Next, we turn the pseudocode into code:

```
function buildFlag()
{
  buildPole();
  buildRectangle();
  comeDown();
}
```

My moveToNextFlag() function is simple; we just need to move twice:

```
function moveToNextFlag()
{
  move();
  move();
}
```

Now let's write the code for buildPole(). We can make the choice along the way—if it is simple enough, we can just write out the code, but if it is too complicated, we can leave it as a function call that we will go and write later. This process of working from the top to the bottom is called **top-down design**.

```
// This function puts 5 balls down in a row
// to build a flagpole
function buildPole()
{
  turnLeft();
  for(var i = 0; i < 5; i++)
  {
    putBall();
    move();
  }
}
```

Then, we can go write buildRectangle() and comeDown():

```
// Create a 3x2 rectangle of tennis balls
function buildRectangle()
{
  putBall();
  move();
  putBall();
  turnRight();
  move();
  putBall();
  move();
  putBall();
  turnRight();
```

```
  move();
  putBall();
  turnRight();
  move();
  putBall();
}


// Bring Karel back to the first row, below
// the end of the flag
function comeDown()
{
  turnLeft();
  for(var i = 0; i < 5; i++)
  {
    move();
  }
  turnLeft();
  move();
}
```

Now we have our completed program. And this allows us to solve the problem as we go. We can start by thinking about the problem in English, breaking it down step by step, then at that point, actually write the code. Here is our full program:

```
move();
buildFlag();
```

```
moveToNextFlag();
buildFlag();
moveToNextFlag();
buildFlag();

// Move twice
function moveToNextFlag()
{
  move();
  move();
}

// Assume we start on the position we want
// to build a flag, on the bottom row
// Assume we end on the bottom row after we
// have built the flag in the rightmost
// position
function buildFlag()
{
  buildPole();
  buildRectangle();
  comeDown();
}

// This function puts 5 balls down in a row
// to build a flagpole
function buildPole()
```

```
{
  turnLeft();
  for(var i = 0; i < 5; i++)
  {
    putBall();
    move();
  }
}

// Create a 3x2 rectangle of tennis balls
function buildRectangle()
{
  putBall();
  move();
  putBall();
  turnRight();
  move();
  putBall();
  move();
  putBall();
  turnRight();
  move();
  putBall();
  turnRight();
  move();
  putBall();
}
```

```
// Bring Karel back to the first row, below
// the end of the flag
function comeDown()
{
  turnLeft();
  for(var i = 0; i < 5; i++)
  {
    move();
  }
  turnLeft();
  move();
}

function turnRight()
{
  turnLeft();
  turnLeft();
  turnLeft();
}
```

TRY IT

Explore a Program

Visit this coding example at
readwritecodebook.com and try to run the
Build Flags program. Try changing the speed
of the program and running one command at
a time.

Problem Decomposition

There are several related concepts here that all help us in
the process of solving our program.

Top-down design is about starting with our problem at
the highest level and then breaking it down into smaller
pieces, bit by bit, until we have smaller problems that are
much more easily solvable.

This is also related to **problem decomposition**—in general, the idea of breaking problems into smaller problems
which are then easier to solve.

And a technique we use along the way is pseudocode,
the idea of writing up your solution to the problem in
something that looks like it's closer to English, so you have
a way to think through your solution to solve it but do not
need to worry about the syntax.

Problem decomposition is a technique you can apply more broadly to all sorts of problems as well as any coding problem.

Say you want to plan an event, like a birthday party. What do you need to do?

Well, you can start by planning at the highest level and then continue to break it down.

To plan a birthday party:
```
Pick a date
Pick a location
Invite guests
Get birthday cake
Celebrate
```

We can then think of the problem and the steps to solve it at this same level, which makes it easier to solve. Then, you could break down each step as necessary to figure out exactly how you do this.

To pick a date:
```
Look at the birthday date
Find a nearby date that is on a weekend
Select that date
```

It may seem silly to break it down in this way, but what is nice about this strategy is it lets you take on very complex

challenges. The reason it works is because you assume
that the functions you made up to call already exist, and
if those smaller parts already exist, then your problem is
solved. You then can go and write those functions later,
but each of those functions is an easier problem.

Say you want to make a movie; what would be the
steps?

```
To make a movie:
Write a script
Get actors
Film movie
Edit movie
```

Now, I'm sure this makes it seem way too easy, but this
lets us abstract away a complex problem into a simple
idea—then we can build it out from there.

Say you wanted to break down the step of filming the
movie; how could you do that?

```
To film a movie:
Schedule film dates
Film scene 1
Film scene 2
Film scene 3
```

How about filming scene 1?

```
To film scene 1:
Set up the set for the location
Get the scene 1 actors
Get the scene 1 props
Run through the scene
```

Now, I'm not exactly sure how they film movies. But what this strategy lets us do is look at a complex problem and think about breaking it down into simple steps all along the way. This is like thinking of the various functions you might write or problems you might solve. This can let you tackle very hard programming problems. An important part of being able to make the simplifications is that you assume each function exists already, and if it does exist, then you've solved your problem. Then, you can go and write that function down later.

Bugs

When you start to write up your programs, you'll find that computers can be very picky. The syntax needs to be just right. It needs to be using words the computer can understand. So, you need to be very detail-oriented. And although you'd like the program to work the first time around, that usually doesn't happen.

When your code doesn't work, doesn't do what you want it to do, or runs into an error, that is called a bug.

In the early days of computers in 1946, while working on the computer the Harvard Mark II, Grace Hopper coined the word "bug." There was actually a moth stuck in the machine, so they removed it. This moth was preventing it from working correctly.

With Karel, you'll see a few types of bugs. When Karel moves but there is a wall in front of them, Karel will crash. So, that's a bug. To avoid this, you need to look at the grid or use conditional statements to make sure the front is clear to move. If Karel takes a ball, but there isn't a ball at that spot, that will also cause an error. Other times, you may want Karel to do one thing, but the program isn't doing what you want. That's also a bug.

People to Know

Grace Hopper was an influential person in the history of computing: she was a computer scientist and Navy admiral and one of the first programmers of the Harvard Mark I computer. She also helped to popularize the idea of programming languages separate from machine language.

Comments

When you write a program, you actually write the code, or the instructions for the computer to execute. Each line needs to be something that the computer can understand. However, as you go, you often want to leave yourself or others reminders or notes of what a particular part of the code is doing or how a function might work. The way you do this is by writing a comment. A **comment** is part of the program but is ignored when the computer is actually running the code. It's a note to yourself, the programmer, or anyone else who may work with the code later. As your programs get more and more complex, it's important to have these comments, so your code becomes easier to understand.

In Karel in JavaScript, you write a single-line comment by adding two slashes at the start of the line then writing your note. The computer will just ignore this part, so this is just a note.

```
// This is a comment
```

Say you want to describe what a function does; you may write something like this:

```
// This function moves Karel 7 spots
// forward.
```

There are a couple ways to write comments; if you want to write a multiline comment in JavaScript, you write it like this:

```
/*
Your comment goes here.
*/
```

Input and Output

Now you've seen the basic building blocks with Karel—and Karel is also in the programming language JavaScript. So, these are also the building blocks of JavaScript. While programming languages can look different or have different parts, they all come back to these basics. There is a lot more advanced material beyond this, but this is how you start.

There are a few other handy concepts in JavaScript, in particular, to know as you navigate the world of coding.

The next idea is input and output. Input is any information you are getting from the user. It could be the user moving their mouse, or it could be them clicking a button or typing something in.

On the flipside, you have output, anything that you are giving back or displaying to the user. So, output would be printing out some text or displaying some graphics on the screen.

Many times, the first program people write in various languages is testing output. You may want to print "Hello world" or anything else out.

Like we showed earlier, to print out "Hello world" you would write this code.

In JavaScript:

```
console.log("Hello world");
```

In Python:

```
print("Hello world")
```

In Java:

```
System.out.println("Hello world");
```

Now, with our new vocabulary, we can recognize that these are all function calls. We are calling a print function or equivalent in the programming language and passing it a parameter of what we want it to print out.

Say you wanted to get user input, like asking the user for their name. You can do that differently in different languages.

In Python:

```
name = input("What's your name? ")
print("Hello " + name)
```

In JavaScript:

```
var name = prompt("What's your name?");
console.log("Hello " + name);
```

In Java:

```
Scanner scanner = new Scanner(System.in);
System.out.println("What's your name? ");
String name = scanner.nextLine();
System.out.println("Hello " + name);
```

As you can see, some languages are easier than others to get started. In Java, for example, I prefer to use another way, which is writing a function to handle the user input for you and abstract away the complexity of using Scanner. So, if you called that, you could write—
    In Java:

```
// This is still Java; it just uses
// functions we already wrote.
// What's nice is you don't have to worry
// about how they work.
String name = input("What's your name? ");
println("Hello " + name);
```

As you'll see, abstraction is a key way of solving problems in programming. You don't need to write everything from scratch, and in reality, nobody does! Everyone is building on components created earlier. Professionals don't program in binary. It's common to use existing libraries all the time. Teachers might see something like this and ask me, "But this isn't how it really works, though, right?" Actually, this is more representative of how it really works.

Variables

Say you wanted to do a math problem in a programming language; it's already supported. So, in JavaScript or Python, you could write:

```
2 + 2
```

And that is a valid line of code. If you printed out or evaluated that expression, it would return 4. But what if you gave me a number and asked me to double it? Say you gave me 10 and asked me to double it; the result would be:

```
10 * 2
```

That is 20. But what if you said, "Double the number 15"? That would be:

```
15 * 2
```

But this isn't very general. How could you make it work for any number you want to double? The way you can do this in programming is by using variables. A **variable** is a way to store a value that you can use later. It usually has a type too—that means it could be a number, letters, or a boolean (true/false). So, in our new program, you would write:

```
num * 2
```

Where num is what you want to double. And if we wanted to get input from the user to ask them, we might write something like this:

```
var num = prompt("What number do you want
    me to double?");
var doubledNumber = num * 2;
```

Here num is a variable, and doubledNumber is a variable. The parts of a variable in JavaScript are a name, a type, and a value.

Name	num
Type	number
Value	5

Name	doubledNumber
Type	number
Value	10

We could then print that out to the screen by writing:

```
console.log(doubledNumber);
```

Again, there's a lot more! But that is the basic info. You may need a number to use later, a number that could change, or a number that you aren't sure what it is yet. You declare a variable as a placeholder for that value and then can store values into it. This is called **assigning to a variable**.

```
Var num = 5;
```

This is how we can assign the variable num the value 5. We could then change it to a new number by updating the value:

```
num = 10;
```

Now that it exists, I don't need to use the word **var**.

Parameters

Now that you know functions and variables, the next thing you can do is understand how you can bring those together with parameters. **Parameters** are the inputs to our function. Basically, a function more generally is something where you can call it but also can give it some inputs, and it will give you something back. I like to imagine functions as a friend who helps you do some random tasks. Say you have a friend named Drake, and he has a hobby where he loves to double numbers. You don't need to know how he does it or what his secret trick is; all you need to know is that you can give him a number (the parameter) and he will give you back the result (the **return value**).

So, a conversation might go like this—this is you and your friend Drake the Doubler.

> **You:** Hey, Drake, can you double a number for me?
> **Drake:** Yes, happy to help here.
> **You:** Drake, can you double the number 7,149?
> **Drake:** The answer is 14,298.
> **You:** Wow, amazing!

Drake is the function, and you can call on him to help you out there. If you were going to code that in JavaScript, here is what you would write:

```
function doubleNumber(x){
  var doubled = x * 2;
  return doubled;
}
```

These are functions just like Karel but also can take inputs, or parameters. Here, the parameter is called x. The way you call, or use, this function is like this:

```
var result = doubleNumber(17);
```

This puts the return value of the function into the variable result.

TRY IT
Double a Number

Visit the examples for this chapter to try out the program to double numbers. Enter a number and see how it works. Now, can you modify this program and function to triple or quadruple a number?

Arrays

Variables let you store values to use for later. And you can create many variables to keep track of these items in your programs.

Say you were tasked to write a program that managed the grades on an exam.

You could store the result of the grade in a variable called **grade** like this:

```
var grade = 90;
```

But say you had two more students. You could then write:

```
var grade2 = 78;
var grade3 = 95;
```

But this doesn't work for very long. What if you had one hundred students? Then, you'd have to write out one hundred variable names. This is where lists, or **arrays**, come in handy. You could create a list to store your grades like this:

```
var grades = [90, 78, 95];
```

Now you can easily access each item in this list. Accessing a particular item is called **indexing**, and these indices start at 0. (Remember, with coding, we usually start at 0.)

So, our array looks like this:

Index	0	1	2
Value	90	78	95

You can access a value in the array like this:

```
grades[0]
```

This gets the first item in the array, which is 90. To save that into a variable, you could write:

```
var studentGrade = grades[0];
```

Say you had a shopping list like this:

```
var groceries = ['apples', 'bananas'];
```

Index	0	1
Value	apples	bananas

You could replace items on the list:

```
groceries[1] = 'oranges';
```

Now you are setting the item at index 1 to oranges.

Index	0	1
Value	apples	oranges

You can also add to the grocery list like this:

```
groceries.push('kiwis');
```

Now your list looks like this:

Index	0	1	2
Value	apples	oranges	kiwis

Objects and Dictionaries

There are many more programming topics to know than we'll cover right here, but this gives you a good handle of the basics. One of the essential data structures that you use very often are lists, or arrays. There is also an important data structure that allows you to store key–value pairs. In different languages, this is called different things, but in JavaScript, they are **objects**, and in Python, they are called **dictionaries**.

An analogy for this is a phone book. A phone book has key–value pairs because you want to store an association. You want to associate a name (the key) with their phone number (the value).

In Python, here is how you might make a phonebook:

```
phonebook = {}
```

Now you can store a number:

```
phonebook['Emergency'] = '911'
```

You can also store another number:

```
phonebook['Jenny'] = '867-5309'
```

You can access a number for a person:

```
jennysNumber = phonebook['Jenny']
```

Now try to print your phonebook:

```
print(phonebook)
{'Emergency': '911', 'Jenny': '867-5309'}
```

Abstraction

Now, in this short little overview of programming concepts, I can share the basics, but it's not enough to make you an expert...yet. But it is enough to hopefully orient you within the world of coding. It's all about building blocks and slowly assembling those building blocks together to make your program.

With our friendly computerized dog Karel, you saw how code is made up of commands and that you can create new commands with functions. You can repeat with loops. You can make decisions with conditional statements. You can break down your problem using top-down design and problem decomposition. You can ask the user for input and display with input and output. You can store numbers for later with variables, and you can give functions inputs with parameters and get back results with return values. You can store lists of values with arrays and key–value mappings with dictionaries or objects. This might be something you could cover in a semester or a year of a first coding class.

But the big ideas are there, and over time, you can get more familiar with them, and you even see them popping up in advanced places. One idea that permeates through the world of code and computer science is abstraction.

Drake, our friend who can double numbers, is an abstraction. I don't have to know how he does it, but I know that he can double numbers. I give him a number, and he doubles it.

With the idea of abstraction and functions, this works no matter how complex the question is.

Say you have another friend Catherine who loves calendars. Drake the Doubler and Catherine the Calendar—all your friends now have special skills and alliterative names. Catherine also has a special skill. You can pick any date, and she can tell you how many days until that date. Say today is July 4, 2020. Here's a conversation between you and Catherine:

> **You:** How many days until July 4, 2030?
> **Catherine:** 3,652.
> **You:** Wow. Okay, how about this one: how many
>   days until January 1, 2065?
> **Catherine:** 16,252.

So, here, the idea is that Catherine is like a function. You can give her a parameter, the date you are asking about, and she somehow magically can figure it out and give you the result.

The idea appears over and over again. You may be writing in a programming language like JavaScript or Python. This is considered a higher-level language. But what's nice about this is that when you are writing in JavaScript, you don't have to know how keyboards work. And you don't have to know how the operating system works. And you don't have to know how the browser draws web pages. Over time, you may want to learn these things to understand it better. But you can work on what you are working on, use the different functions or tools, or libraries or APIs available to you, and abstract away the actual details of how they work. Each programming language also comes with its set of built-in functions, just like Karel.

If you can internalize this idea, it's very powerful. It means you can pick up a library or function that someone else wrote and use it in your code without having to know exactly how that works. This is the same thing as when you do top-down design in Karel. If you can abstract some of those problems away, you can think about solving the problem at the level that you are at.

So, while Karel is a friendly way to start, from there, you can build up all the programming basics and start to practice and apply these concepts.

5
Data, the Cloud, and Open Source

1001010101101000101010100010101001010101010101010111010101100101010010101010100101010010101

Early on in CodeHS, we accidentally deleted almost all the data on our site. Our mistake deleted the user accounts, the classes, the courses, and most of the data in our database. We had wanted to delete *one* thing, but instead, the site stopped working. We definitely freaked out, but luckily, we didn't just have one copy of the database. It was backed up using the cloud. This means that within a few hours, we were able to restore the site to what it was a before.

Digital Data

In computing, **data** is just a sequence of bits. On its own, it doesn't mean anything. But that data can become information when you know how to interpret it.

A number is data, a word can be data, but so can a group of a million numbers or a million words.

A program itself is data. This is a bit of a confusing concept, but the bits that make up the instructions for the computer to process data are also data.

When you make a phone call, the sound you make is turned into data that can then be sent and interpreted. When you make a purchase on a site, a transaction is logged. Anything you do on a computer generates data. An image file is data; an e-book is data; a tweet, a timestamp, an email, and a calendar invite are data. A click, a location, a rating, and a review are data. It can then be processed, transformed, sent, saved, used, or even misused. But it's important to see that the digital world is a factory for churning out data.

Many of the large tech businesses, like Google, Facebook, and Amazon, run on data. The data they have includes consumer purchases, searches, friends, likes, clicks, downloads, locations, and more.

On your computer or your phone, your data in storage is on a hard drive or solid-state drive. But so much of your data is not on your own devices anymore. It lives on a database or, really, in the cloud.

Databases

So, you start with 1s and 0s. You build up to bits and bytes, then megabytes and gigabytes. But then what? You can store files like you do on your own computer. But how does a website store your information?

Websites store information about the users, the accounts, and everything else in databases. If you've used a spreadsheet, a **database** is like a really big spreadsheet. Say you have your own website, and the website has user accounts. Each row in your big spreadsheet, or each row in your database, represents a user with an account. Then, each column in the spreadsheet represents something you want to store, like their name, their email, or their username. And that really is what a database is. It might be huge—it might store millions or billions of users—but that is what a database is.

A database itself is a software application; some well-known database applications are MySQL or Postgres. They handle figuring out how to store and retrieve the data efficiently. They've abstracted the problem away, and they give you functions to work with or an API that lets you store information or retrieve it later. You can write a database query, which is when you ask a question of the database.

For example, you might want to ask, "Can you get the information for user number 5?"

What might that look like if you wrote the query? **SQL** is a query language, a programming language that lets you interface with databases. You might have something like this:

```
SELECT * FROM UserTable WHERE ID = 5;
```

The words with all capital letters are the keywords, or special words that mean something specific in the query language. `UserTable` is the name of our database table, or big spreadsheet, which stores all of the information. ID is the column, or the field of the database, and we are just looking for user number 5.

That might return something like this:

```
UserTable
ID | first_name | last_name | username        |
5  | Jeremy     | Keeshin   | jeremykeeshin   |
```

This is what a database is. So, you have data in a database...when it gets really big, there are all sorts of tools to process it, visualize it, and transform it.

For our site at CodeHS, we use a MySQL database, which has hundreds of tables, and one of those tables stores the information for user accounts like this. Our database table has millions of rows since we have millions of users on our site. We have an ID field too—this is very common to have a number like ID as an easy way to uniquely identify a row.

Big Data

So, now that you know data and databases...what is big data? How big does it need to be to qualify as "big data"? Any action you do can be a data point. When you move around with your phone, it tracks your GPS location all the time. Your phone tracks this thousands of times a day... but it does this for everyone who has location tracking. So, what happens when you aggregate this among lots of people? This is big data. Aggregating data points across millions or billions of users is big data.

On Google, there are 40,000 searches per second, about 4 billion searches per day, and over 1 trillion searches per year. This is big data. When you have this whole new level of data—beyond gigabytes, beyond terabytes—the implications are very different. The questions become: how is the data analyzed, how is it used to power different algorithms and AI, and how is it monitored, stored, and deleted?

Big data is much of what enables and powers the new information economy. But with big data comes lots of risks as well. How is this data collected? Is it clear what is collected? Many people do not realize what is collected about them, and it can even be considered heavy surveillance. First, where is the data stored?

What Is the Cloud?

You may have heard of "the cloud" when referring to other websites. What is the cloud? It's a pretty general term—it's definitely a tech term, but it's not the clouds in the sky. So, what is it?

The cloud very broadly refers to types of software applications that don't live on your computer but usually live on the servers of a company, and you access them through your web browser. This means that instead of needing to re-download an application or save your files to your computer, they are saved somewhere else on the internet, so you can access them.

If you have a file on your computer, and you lose or break your computer, then that file is gone. So, file storage was a natural application for the cloud. A company and application, like Dropbox, store your files in the cloud—essentially, just on their computers. This is the same with Google Drive or iCloud.

One clear benefit of the cloud is it makes things easier for the user. You don't have to worry about backing things up since it saves automatically. This also means that you have access to more storage space or more computing power than you may have on your own device. The way many of these apps work is you can interact with them through a website, but then they can do the heavy lifting on their own servers.

One tradeoff of storing things in the cloud is that your data is somewhere else, which means it isn't fully under your control.

Where Is the Cloud?

Now, you may be wondering: where is the cloud? That is a great question. If you went to look for the cloud, what you would end up finding is that, really, the cloud lives in various warehouses all over the world—these warehouses are called data centers. Data centers have tons of computers and are hooked up to the internet, and this is where many things get stored.

So, the cloud is really just lots of computers all over the place—but like a server, it is usually on someone else's computer.

But if you are a company, you may be managing your own cloud—really, just managing your own servers and hardware that serve as the behind-the-scenes technology powering your website or application.

What's nice now is that if you are building your own website, you don't have to create your own server setup and data center; you can use existing data centers and servers. For example, at CodeHS, our servers run on AWS, so we are using Amazon's cloud—just meaning we are taking advantage of the computer setup that Amazon has to run our apps, so we don't have to set that up.

So, why is it called "the cloud"? The cloud was used as a metaphor for the internet and appeared in diagrams or networks of computers early on. Partly, the cloud metaphor meant that you didn't have to worry about the underlying details.

AWS

Why is AWS worth mentioning here? And what is AWS? In the acronym-filled world of learning about computing, why is this one worth knowing? **AWS** stands for Amazon Web Services. It's the name of Amazon's cloud computing services and business. There are lots and lots of products as part of AWS. AWS is a very popular provider of cloud computing. Essentially, when you want to get your servers but maybe not manage them yourselves, AWS is a very popular option.

Our site for CodeHS is all built on AWS, which is where we then have our servers, our databases, and much more.

Data Centers

"The cloud" is this amorphous idea—it's the ether; it's the web; it's out there somewhere else that isn't here. But the cloud is an idea. However, it does have a physical presence, and the clearest way to see that is in a data center. But a data center, in reality, may have the opposite feel of the ethereal idea of the cloud.

So, what is a **data center** like now? It can be a building or complex where they keep lots of computers and everything else needed to run them. If the cloud is someone else's computer, the data center is where some big companies house tons of their computers. But their computers may have very different requirements than a computer or laptop that you use. For example, on your own computer, you have a monitor, but computers in a data center won't need monitors. A data center will have rows and rows of computers. They have server racks, which is a stack of computers on one particular configuration.

Anything you do with a computer generates data, and as that data proliferates, it needs somewhere to go.

There are lots of different types of data centers, but the ones hosted by Facebook or Amazon actually power the sites and save lots of the images and other data.

One challenge in data centers is the temperature since having so many computers in one place generates so much heat.

Open Source Software

Wherever there is technology, we can always look for two different parts: the software and the hardware. The hardware is the physical part, like your laptop or phone or even a server rack in a data center. The software is the code that is running, including the apps, the programs, and the websites.

There's an important category of software to know about. While much of the software might be written by a particular company—and is proprietary, so you won't have access to it—there is a lot of **open source software**, where the software is shared, accessible, and available, often for free. There are various open source licenses, but some let you use that software for free and do whatever you want with it, including even resell it.

What's fascinating is that so much of the software you use every day is powered by open source software under the hood. This is because open source makes up the foundational layer of many operating systems, libraries, and programming languages. In addition, because it's open and free, this helps contribute to its popularity.

For example, the Linux operating system is open source. This means you can see the code and even contribute to it.

Today, you can find the code at this URL: *https://github.com/torvalds/linux.*

People to Know

Linux was created by Linus Torvalds, a Finnish and American open source software developer. He's also the creator of Git, which is version control software.

There are many different versions of Linux; some popular ones include Debian, Fedora, and Ubuntu. Linux also has commercial distributions like Red Hat. It is also the most popular operating system for servers. And this was all created and given away for free by people contributing voluntarily.

It's a whole new work model and one that is crucial to understanding the internet.

The Left-Pad Bug

What I hope you'll get as you continue through this book is the experience of filling in the pieces to a jigsaw puzzle. As you place each additional puzzle piece, it's a bit clearer how it all fits together.

Now, I want to tell you about the left-pad bug and how it broke many sites on the internet and major projects stopped working. You now have the pieces to understand it, which are: bugs, strings, JavaScript, and open source software.

A programmer named Azer Koçulu deleted eleven lines of code in a small unknown library. His library was called left-pad, and it added characters to the start of a string.

Suddenly, tons of projects all over were breaking—and people didn't even know what left-pad is! How did this happen?

Here is the left-pad function:

```
module.exports = leftpad;
function leftpad (str, len, ch) {
  str = String(str);
  var i = -1;
  if (!ch && ch !== 0) ch = ' ';
  len = len - str.length;
  while (++i < len) {
    str = ch + str;
  }
  return str;
}
```

This function adds characters to the left of a string, which could be spaces or any other character. For example, this function call adds eight spaces to the front, so the string is ten characters long.

```
leftpad("hi", 10) → "hi"
```

This small library was an open source piece of software that many people could use and was a dependency of lots of software projects. This means lots of projects included it as part of their project, and when they would be created, they would pull in that package. Suddenly, that package disappeared, and people got an error.

How could people use a package without knowing it? Projects have a list of packages and libraries they use, some they have written, but many are open source packages which people get online. There is a registry of JavaScript packages called npm, which hosted this package. So, people may have a list of ten packages, but those packages may depend on packages, which may depend on packages, and so on. So, somewhere along the line...a lot of people were using left-pad, and major projects broke!

What this underscores is that major projects (and likely, almost every website or piece of software you use) depend on open source software. It may be behind the scenes, but no one is writing everything from scratch. Because of the abstraction, people build their systems on top of other existing systems.

Git and GitHub

Linus Torvalds, the eponymous creator of Linux, is also the main author of another widely used piece of open source software: Git. Git is a version control system, which allows you to save and track different versions of the code you are creating with a lot of different people. This turns out to be very helpful as you build a big project like Linux, an operating system.

For example, if you are working on an essay, you may want to create multiple versions. Say you have an essay you are working on called:

Essay.doc

You make some edits, and now, you have version 2:

Essay2.doc

You send that to your friend, who edits it and renames it:

Essay2-edited.doc

But now, you have another friend, who edits it and says, This is now the final draft:

Essay2-edited-FINAL.doc

But then, you realize there are more edits, and you also date the file:

Essay2-edited-FINAL-02-05-2020.doc

You can see that this quickly gets hard to track. Now, imagine you are doing this with lots of people, maybe even hundreds of people, with lots of files, but with code. When you are working on software at a company, with a group, or even with an open source project, you need a way to coordinate among people. You need to be able to work on different features, be able to save your changes, and combine your changes with others.

This is similar to the workflow of editing an essay or even editing versions of a legal document, but because it's code, it has a lot more technical capabilities. You can save a version in what is called a **commit**. You can then create a new version that you want to work on by creating a **branch**. And you can send your code up to a shared repository by using a command called **push**, get code from other people with a command called **pull**, and update your version with a command called **merge**. There's a lot more, but those are the basics.

There is a popular site called GitHub (*github.com*), which hosts Git repositories. You can see that lots of open source software is there and easily view the code or even make your own version of it (called **forking**). There's a whole lingo of open source software, but it's powerful to know and understand how it works, and you can really peek under the hood as much as you want. Even the code for the website for this book is open source on GitHub! Check it out under the links for this chapter at *readwritecodebook.com*.

Issues to Know: Location Tracking

Now, say you operate a mapping software app like Google Maps. You store locations, and you store user accounts. You let people store their favorite places and search for things. You need to have a database to store all this data.

Now, say you come up with a handy feature, as Google Maps has, to store all the places you've been and that you've searched. This way, you can easily go find places you've already searched or been to. It would be convenient.

Now, what if your phone is on all the time, and you carry it with you, and it actually stores your location every second because then it can automatically find the places you go, and you can figure out where you've been? Now, that is interesting but also raises some questions.

Now, what if they can track everywhere you go, all the time, but then can do that for a billion people—what about that? This seems like a lot. This is also the state of things today.

What does this data mean? What does this data mean for an individual? What does it mean in aggregate? What can I find out about people that they may not realize? How is this data managed, organized, and deleted? Can I see a copy of my data? What if the government requests the data?

These are some of the thorny issues around data collection and data privacy that it is past time that the country and world start to figure out. Right now, the answer to these questions is concerning, and there aren't enough controls on what can be done.

Now, what if you use another app (say a weather app, a reviews app, or another random app), and it ostensibly uses your location to provide you a service, like show you the weather in your current location. But now, that location data is collected from you all the time, even though you may have thought they only needed it here and there just to show you the weather. And now this random weather app knows all of your location data. But the real problem here is now this app takes the data and resells it to other marketing data and analytics companies that want to understand consumer behavior and retarget ads to you. Did you know that your location was being used this way? Would you have downloaded and used this weather app if they told you right up front how they were using the data? These are the questions that are very relevant to the privacy setup of your phones.

There are very real tradeoffs to collecting data, keeping data, and deleting data. The cloud provides us a lot of conveniences, like keeping a backup of the CodeHS database when we accidentally deleted it many years ago. But there are also risks to data storage and collection that need to be considered.

6
Cybersecurity and Cryptocurrency

100101010101101000101010100010101010101001010101010101010101010110101011001010010010101010010101010101101010101

Falling for Scams

I've fallen for a few scams, and I've also had some close calls. The internet has opened a whole new world for scammers, so you have to be careful. I've become much more skeptical both online and in-person as I've learned more.

When I was in high school, I had a close call where I tried to buy a Segway on eBay from a guy in Bucharest, Romania, who wanted me to send money through Western Union. In hindsight, this is just amusing to me, but I'm sure then I was convinced I had found a good deal.

Once in college, I bought a fake winning lottery ticket at a gas station from someone who said he needed gas money. In hindsight, did the story make sense? Not really. But I bought the story as they told me how much I was helping them. I looked at the lottery ticket, which seemed like a real winning ticket to me as well as the gas station attendant. And it turned out it was real; it had just already been redeemed.

Once, I was traveling in Thailand in Bangkok, and we were going to see the Grand Palace. On the way over, a young Thai man stopped us and explained that the Grand Palace was closed until 2 p.m. since it was Buddha Day on Saturday. Well, when he explained that, it seemed totally reasonable. Instead of that, he said we could go to see a bunch of other places in a small open taxi, a tuk-tuk, for very cheap. So, we got into the tuk-tuk.

A couple minutes in, I remembered that I had read online earlier that day about a tuk-tuk scam where they got you into a tuk-tuk for cheap, then took you around to other places...wait a second. I googled "Bangkok scams," and the first result that came up detailed a scam that began exactly the way this interaction had. So, we got out of the tuk-tuk and avoided the scam. The Grand Palace was not closed, and there was no Buddha Day. But lots of tourists fall for these types of shady tricks, and the scammers are good.

The scammers in the digital world are cunning and clever as well, and you need to learn a few tricks and stay alert.

Cybersecurity

Cybersecurity is in the news more than ever now. As technology is used across so many parts of society, protecting these systems from bad actors becomes an even more important and more difficult task. **Cybersecurity** is protecting computer systems from attacks of various kinds. This could mean protecting the hardware, the data, or another part of the system. There are many different types of attacks; we will look at a few of the different attacks and why this is such a tough problem.

One reason this is such a hard problem is because, to break into a system, an attacker might just need one tiny vulnerability, or a weakness or error in the system. But to keep a system secure you will need to account for every possibility and every area it could be attacked.

Hacking

More and more, you'll see "hacking" in the news. But what does that really mean? Okay, someone was hacked, but what are the implications, and how did that happen?

Hacking means that someone got unauthorized access to some computer system. This could mean that an attacker found a vulnerability in the system and may have taken it over. If a system was hacked, that means someone got access and may have been able to get some data they weren't supposed to get. But various types of attacks make up hacking today. It may be an attack to take down a system.

Here are a few types of attacks to know about:

- A **botnet** is when an entity controls a network of computers that it may use for an attack.

- A **denial of service (DoS)** or **distributed denial of service (DdoS) attack** is one where a hacker tries to take down a site by overwhelming the site with traffic. In a DdoS attack, the traffic is coming from many sources, so it may be harder to prevent.

- A **ransomware attack** is one where malicious software is installed on a computer, which then encrypts the data or files, making it unusable, and the attacker demands a ransom to provide the secret key that will unlock and restore the usage of the files.

Recently, in the news, there have been many reported data breaches. This means a hacker got access to a system, and personal information was revealed or released. Data breaches could release names, phone numbers, addresses, billing details, or payment information. Now, data breaches and hacking are so common that you cannot really trust that the information you are giving to websites is private. In 2019 alone, about 8 billion records were exposed in data breaches. For context, there are about 8 billion people in the world.

Phishing

From: Your Friend <notreallytheiremail@gmail.com>
Sent: Monday, May 25, 2020 3:12 PM
To: Reader <youremail@gmail.com>

I need to get three iTunes gift cards for my niece. It's her birthday, but I can't do this now because I'm currently traveling. Can you get them for me from any store around you? I'll pay back next week when I get back home.

You receive an email like this, which looks like it's sent by your friend who needs help getting a gift card for their niece. Looks reasonable? Look again. This is a phishing email.

Have you ever received an email that seemed a little bit...fishy? Asking you for personal information, urging a particular response, sending you to an unfamiliar link, asking you to buy something or pay someone, or any number of other variations?

This is called a phishing email or phishing attack. **Phishing** is where an attacker or bad actor tries to obtain your personal information by fooling you into thinking they are someone else, or to enter your information on a site that isn't what it says it is.

It may start as an email that impersonates someone you know or impersonates a company you are connected with. It may then ask you to reply with information, ask you to enter information on a site, or ask you to log in but on a fake page that takes your login info.

It's a very tricky practice, and mostly, it works by trying to deceive you. It's possible for anyone to fall for this, even if you are an experienced tech user.

How can you protect against phishing or falling for this scam yourself? There are a few things to know that can help.

Learn about Phishing

You've taken one big step now—you know about phishing. The more you know about what it is and how an attacker may try to fool you will help you identify and prevent bad scenarios.

Another thing to do is just slow down: if you get an email that seems suspicious to you, you want to be careful with any of the links, attachments, and entering information on sites that it links to.

Look for Warning Signs

Phishing attacks broadly use common tactics including appeals to persuasion from authority, financial gain or loss messaging, and emotional salience. There are lots of types of phishing attacks, from high volume to very targeted. A tactic may be a spoofed email from your boss asking you to do something quickly. The high urgency is a tactic common to phishing. It may offer something free, or a refund, or a coupon, or scare you into thinking that you might lose something if you don't take action. You may see emails with lots of typos, or it may refer to or address you with generic information. They may ask you to buy gift cards like our example above. Phishing tactics evolve, but when you see something off, slow down and take another look.

Check the Domain

Next, you want to always check the URL of the site you are looking at. Say you receive a phishing email from your bank. While your bank may have a domain like this:

wellsfargo.com

A phishing attack may take you to a site that looks very similar but isn't the same, like:

wellsfargo.com.phishingsite.com/login

This is actually a *subdomain* of *phishingsite.com*, not *wellsfargo.com*, so if you only glance at the URL, you could get fooled. You can also check in your URL bar to see if the site is secure. So, in summary, you need to double check that the site you are on is actually the site you think you are on. As simple as this sounds, this is an easy step to miss. Someone could create a page that looks exactly like the Google home page or login and fool you into entering your password there. If they do that, then they can steal your passwords and take over your accounts.

Check the Email of the Sender

Next, check that the email is actually from who you think it's from. Email has a lot of insecure components to it, and one thing many people do not realize is you can create an email and send it saying your email address is...anything. You may see an email come in that says it is from me:

Jeremy Keeshin *<myemail@gmail.com>*

But you could have received an email where someone just changed the display name, and it instead is:

Jeremy Keeshin *<attackeremail@gmail.com>*

Sometimes only the display name shows. You can click more information on your email to see the full email address of the sender. If the email address is someone else impersonating the person sending the message, that is likely a scam. In addition, while someone could spoof certain parts, like the name or even the address, the originating server is harder to spoof. So, if you go and see the full email information, you can see if it's signed properly or not. In many cases, an email client like Gmail can warn you if a message looks suspicious, but many of these factors, it won't find yet.

Be Careful with Passwords

Oftentimes, the attacker may be trying to take over personal information or your login information. In particular, you need to be careful with passwords. If someone has your password, they can log in to your account. So, be careful of where you enter your password. Additionally, you don't want to share your password. If you have a site that asks for your password, again, double-check the domain and that it's actually the site you want to use.

Identity Theft

With these data breaches, it's important to know about identity theft and how you can prevent it. Identity theft would be someone taking over information about your identity through public, private, or hacked information and then using that to impersonate you and complete fraudulent actions. This could be someone stealing your credit card, getting credit cards or loans, trying to take someone else's tax refund, or using it in various ways.

Passwords

To log in to a system, you'll usually need your username or email and password. Soon, you'll see how you can make this more secure. Your username may be public on the site you are on, but your password is secret. So, your password is the secret key that gets you into a website.

First, you want to keep your password safe and secure. But with the proliferation of accounts and hacks, how can you even keep track of your passwords and accounts? With password management, there are many pitfalls but also some best practices you should know.

Here are a few of the challenges you may have already run into:

- It can be hard to keep track of accounts. What sites do you have an account on?
- It can be hard to remember all your passwords.

You could be using the same password everywhere, which is one of the bigger problems. This means if any site you have an account on gets hacked, and the passwords were stored in plain text, then they can use your username and password to log in to your other accounts.

You could have lots of different passwords but have a hard time remembering which ones are for which site. You might have some written down somewhere, some in another place, or some you are always forgetting or needing to reset.

There are two main tips I recommend for passwords:

- One is ensuring password length is long enough.
- The other is a password system.

There are a few variations of each, but I think it's helpful to understand why these help.

There are often tradeoffs when it comes to thinking about improving security. The tradeoffs usually come in the form of security versus convenience. While a certain system or method may be more secure, it may also be more inconvenient. However, a system that is maybe the most secure, if unused because it is so inconvenient, isn't helping you either.

If someone is going to hack into one of your accounts, there are a few different ways this might be done:

- Reusing data released in a data breach on other sites
- Dictionary attack
- Brute force attack
- Rainbow table
- Phishing
- Social engineering
- Guessing

Avoid Password Reuse

One way you could be hacked is if your account information is released in a data breach, and you use the same password and username on many sites. A hacker then can simply try this password on other sensitive accounts. This one is completely preventable, and you can protect yourself!

Many of these attackers may try to overtake accounts en masse, which means by unlinking the account information, you've improved your security. It is different if they are going for your account in particular, but protecting against the easy cases really helps.

To protect against this, you either need:

- Different emails/usernames on every site
- Different passwords on every site
- Both different usernames and different passwords

While different emails/usernames and different passwords is this most secure, this is the hardest to do. I have set up a system where I can create one-off email addresses that go to me for any site, but this requires more setup. Additionally, it can be harder to remember various usernames or emails, and in many sites, your username may be visible. So, while this is the most secure, it is harder to do.

Creating different passwords on different sites, however, is much easier to do and is an essential security step. You can use randomly generated passwords, but then you can't remember those. If you do use randomly generated passwords, either by your browser or by a program, you will likely need a password manager to organize those. A **password manager** is a program that lets you organize your passwords. It keeps track of your account information, like username and password, for every site and autofills it in for you. You don't actually need to remember your individual site passwords, but you remember one main master password. Now, one inconvenience here is you don't actually know your passwords so need to practice using the password manager.

Another system which I like is using a rule to generate your password. This works in the form of having a base password and then some additional password component or transformation that varies by site. Now this accomplishes a couple of things. It's more convenient because you can know your passwords. It also prevents against keeping your account information linked since your password on each site is unique. The reason this is effective is because it prevents common attacks that take advantage of password reuse, and if one site is compromised, none of your other sites are.

This may run into a roadblock when sites have conflicting password rules (these aren't helping anyone), so you need to account for that. This is when a site says a password must be a certain number of characters long or have uppercase or lowercase letters or special characters or numbers.

Here's how this system might work:

Pick some base password that you have. Say my base password is "colorful." Then, add some numbers like "904."

Then, pick a rule based on the name of the site. Say my rule was to take the first three letters. So, if the site was Google, I could take "goo" or "GOO." If the site was Wikipedia, I could add "wik" or "WIK."

Then you can combine these in various ways. You could start by doing the component related to the site, then a number, then your base password.

So, your Google password might be:

gooCOLORFUL904

And Wikipedia might be:

wikCOLORFUL904

What is much better about this than a system that uses the same password everywhere is you can remember it, but you have also unlinked your passwords from each other, so if one account is compromised, it does not compromise the others.

Some people also like **passphrases**, which are long but memorable phrases that either are used entirely or you just can take the first letter. So, it may look random but is easy to remember.

A passphrase could be something like this:

roundish sloppily zone guidance

This now gives you a 31-character password, which is very hard to guess. To crack this password would take 25.48 billion trillion trillion centuries to search all possibilities at 100 billion guesses per second.

Say you generate a password of random characters:

Y2y1qd4HDepMVQ8hGM4F

This is very hard to remember. This would take 2.28 thousand trillion centuries at 100 billion guesses per second.

You could also use a password padding setup (a variation of the rule-based system) to lengthen your password but keep it easy to remember. Say you had the word "egg"; you could have a password where you add the same character many times to make it longer:

Egg2!**************

Which is the word "egg," capitalized, the number 2, an exclamation point, and fifteen asterisks. This password is even more secure—11.52 thousand trillion centuries to break via brute force—and the same number of characters. Even though it has a simpler format and is easier to remember for you, an attacker still has to search all combinations.

Prevent Hackers from Guessing Your Password

So, why does any of this help? Well, out of some of the main ways you might be attacked, it's most likely to occur as a data breach or some sort of dictionary or brute force attack. An attacker trying to guess could try one of these techniques.

A **dictionary attack** would be if a hacker just goes through words in a dictionary or some wordlist and tries all of those as your password. Unfortunately, people might just pick lots of regular words. And these can be guessed and broken quickly. Someone could attempt a **brute force attack**, which doesn't just go through words in the dictionary but any combination of letters so trying variations including letters, numbers, and characters. Or they might just try to guess. If you have a longer password, one that is different per site and not just a dictionary or common password, you significantly make it harder to crack.

In some cases, if they have the database of passwords, but they are all hashed, then they can run a program offline looking at the hashes. A **rainbow table attack** is one where they have precomputed the hashes of passwords, which will speed up looking at the hashes.

That is a summary, but understanding the math behind it also makes it clear why this is the case.

Here's a question: how long does it take to crack your password that you might use on Facebook, Google, Instagram, or Snapchat?

Think of your password. Now think of the length of it and what kinds of characters are in it.

Now remember back to for `loops` and `while` loops. Loops let us repeat code. And computers can run code very quickly. What if you had a program with pseudocode that looked like this:

```
While have not guessed the password
   Come up with the next guess
   If the guess is right
      Done
```

The computer can do this very fast. It depends on a number of factors, but it could guess over a hundred million or even billions of passwords per second. If they are trying this on a site, it depends on the rate limit set by the website, but it could be thousands of guesses per second.

This table breaks down how long it would take to do a brute force search of all the possible password combinations. The alphabet is how many possible letters are in your password. The search space size is how many possible combinations there are. "Lower" means the 26 lowercase letters. "Upper" means the 26 uppercase letters. "Digits" means the numbers 0–9. So, "Lower, Upper" has an alphabet size of 52 (26 + 26).

Exact numbers depend on the scenario, but you could see how a five-letter password takes a split second to crack, and at ten upper and lowercase characters with an online attack, it would take 46,000 centuries to break. At fifteen characters with uppercase, lowercase, and digits, it would take 2.44 million centuries to crack at 100 billion guesses per second. So, you are better off adding a few extra letters than trying to come up with something really complicated.

Name	Alphabet Size	Length	Search Space	Time to Crack (1k/second)	Time to Crack (100B/second)
Lower	26	5	11,881,376	3.3 hours	0.000119 seconds
Lower, Upper	52	5	380,204,032	4.4 days	0.003802 seconds
Lower, Upper, Digits	62	5	916,132,832	10.6 days	0.009161 seconds
Lower, Upper, Digits, Special	95	5	7,737,809,375	2.99 months	0.077378 seconds
Lower	26	10	1.41e+14	44.76 centuries	23.53 minutes
Lower, Upper	52	10	1.45e+17	45.84 thousand centuries	16.73 days
Lower, Upper, Digits	62	10	8.39e+17	266.14 thousand centuries	3.24 months
Lower, Upper, Digits, Special	95	10	5.99e+19	18.99 million centuries	18.99 years
Lower	26	15	1.68e+21	531.86 million centuries	5.32 centuries
Lower, Upper	52	15	5.50e+25	1743 trillion centuries	174.28 thousand centuries
Lower, Upper, Digits	62	15	7.69e+26	243.82 trillion centuries	2.44 million centuries
Lower, Upper, Digits, Special	95	15	4.63e+29	1.47e+5 trillion centuries	1.47 billion centuries
Lower	26	20	1.99e+28	6.32e+3 trillion centuries	63.19 million centuries
Lower, Upper	52	20	2.09e+34	6.63e+9 trillion centuries	66.26 trillion centuries
Lower, Upper, Digits	62	20	7.04e+35	2.23e+11 trillion centuries	2.23e+3 trillion centuries
Lower, Upper, Digits, Special	95	20	3.58e+39	1.14e+15 trillion centuries	1.14e+7 trillion centuries

The main takeaway from the table is that the most important factor is the length.

Preventing Phishing and Social Engineering

One other concern with passwords is giving them to the wrong people and wrong sites. While this sounds simple, in practice, it can be very tricky.

We looked at phishing earlier—often, the end result of a phishing attack is that the attacker may be trying to get your password. We looked at a few ways they might try to get your password: through a data breach, hacking another system, or even by guessing directly through a brute force or dictionary attack. But another way to get your password is to get it directly from you.

Yes, it does sound a bit silly to think you would give the attacker your password directly. But phishing can be really tricky.

In general, there is an attack method called **social engineering**. The way this works is that instead of taking advantage of a technical vulnerability in the system, they try to manipulate the different people in it.

Have you received a spam phone call telling you that you had an issue with the IRS? Or someone pretending to be your bank and wasn't? Or a call from India telling you that you have a virus? These would all be social engineering scams. They could be a step in trying to get you to divulge certain information or access.

Phishing is a type of social engineering attack.

Someone could call up the support line of a website that you use, pretend to be you, and try to use publicly available information or information they gathered to convince the support person to reset your password or give access to your account. People also have done this attack to try to take over cell phone numbers, which provides another method of taking over accounts.

A social engineering attack could be having someone call into an office pretending to be the IT person and asking directly for the password. Or someone writing or impersonating that they need to have some funds transferred, an opportunity in Nigeria, or asking you to buy gift cards.

At CodeHS, we actually have people regularly receive phishing emails; some are emails impersonating me, asking other team members to do something. We do trainings on security, but even with that, it can still be a challenge.

How can you prevent these types of social engineering attacks? First, be careful not to share your password. If someone asks you for your password in an email or on a phone call, that is a red flag. In general, you want to have your own password for your own user account, not shared passwords. When you receive an email for a request for information or to click a link that seems suspicious, double-check the sender, the domain, and the destination of the URL. When you are on a website, make sure it's the site you think it is by checking the domain. You can also check that it is secure by looking at the URL bar. Don't type your password into a site that is not the site you are trying to use. When asked for a strange request of information, slow down or even check to verify manually with the person if the request was real. Those can often be scams.

Two-Factor Authentication

So, now, with all that we know about some of the possible security issues (and there are a lot more) and some of the issues and vulnerabilities with passwords, what else can we do to secure our accounts? Is making a long password that is different on every site all we can do? No.

A key step in securing your accounts is both enabling and using two-factor authentication.

When you log in with just a password, that is just one factor, or way to show you are who you say you are.

Two-factor authentication means that to get into your account, you need two factors. This is usually something you know, like a password, and something you have, like your phone.

How would this work more specifically? You can download a two-factor authentication app (sometimes written 2FA) like Google Authenticator. Then, while logged into your account, say a Google account, you connect your app to the account by scanning a QR code. A **QR code** is usually a box with black and white squares that has information like a number or a link. Now that your app is hooked up, it will start to generate random six-digit numbers that change every thirty seconds.

Now you have a new login flow for your accounts:

- Go to a website login page
- Enter your username and password
- Now you are prompted for a two-factor authentication code
- Open up Google Authenticator and look for the code corresponding to your site
- Enter in the code

So, there are two big steps:

1. Enter your password
2. Enter your two-factor authentication code

This is much more secure. The codes from Google Authenticator are considered OTPs (one-time passwords) since they just work right then for your account.

The reason this is more secure is that even if my password was hacked, phished, or in a data breach, the attacker would then go to the site to try to take over my account, and while they would successfully get my password, they would then be prompted to enter my 2FA code. But they don't have that! Since they need my phone to get that. So, as long as I have my phone, I have an additional level of security. Now, if they got your phone, that would be a problem.

There are less secure 2FA formats like SMS-based 2FA, meaning you send the code in a text message. Wherever possible, do not use SMS 2FA. This is susceptible to a SIM swap attack, where an attacker can take over your phone number by social engineering the phone company; this happens a lot and is a really bad scam.

If your second factor is a text, but someone else can get your texts, that is a problem. With the authenticator app, they need your actual phone to get your 2FA code.

Practical Security Tips

Here are a few tips as a summary.

Passwords

- Use passwords at least ten characters long, with numbers and upper and lowercase letters. Even longer is better.
- The length matters much more than the complexity in preventing a brute force or dictionary attack.
- You can use a password manager or come up with a rule that makes sure you have different passwords on different sites.

Phishing and Social Engineering

- Attackers may try to fool you into giving them your information directly to take over your password, account, or steal your identity. Be careful to double-check the email sender, domain, and any links in the email.
- Make sure you double-check the URL of the site where you enter your password, looking for a secure icon from the browser.

Two-Factor Authentication

- Make sure to set up two-factor authentication on your major accounts since this greatly increases the security. I strongly recommend making sure you have 2FA on your email account since, if someone takes over your email, they can easily take over other accounts.
- SMS-based two-factor authentication is not secure and can be hacked via SIM swap social engineering attacks.
- You can use an app like Google Authenticator to manage two-factor authentication. You need to have backups if you lose your phone.

Cryptocurrency and Blockchain

Now, let's zoom over to a different (but related) area to talk about cryptocurrency and blockchain.

Some of the building blocks of the web are that it is distributed, meaning there isn't a single person that owns it. Anyone can put up a page on the web. However, most money systems are controlled by a central bank. This means the government can print and issue new money. What if the internet had money built in, that was distributed, and that nobody owned but anyone could use? That's part of the idea behind Bitcoin.

In the internet chapter, we talked about HTTP and HTTPS as protocols. With HTTPS, the data is encrypted, so it cannot be intercepted along the way. When it's encrypted, it is encrypted using cryptography. **Cryptography** is the study of how to do secure communication and includes various parts of math, computer science, and physics, creating ciphers, codes, and more.

Cryptocurrency is digital money that is secured by cryptography and distributed, so there isn't one person who controls it.

So, a cryptocurrency is an online virtual currency; it's like the digital version of cash. It's not physical like a ten-dollar bill. But it's not controlled just by one bank or by a government. It's secured by a distributed set of **nodes**, or computers on the network. They all have a copy of the transactions and balances, which make up the ledger. This ledger is called the blockchain.

Ah! So many new words, it's hard to keep track.

What's important to remember is:

- Cryptocurrency is online digital currency
- It's distributed; there isn't one person who owns it
- It's secured by cryptography (or math)
- Anyone who wants can have a whole entire copy of the full ledger

The security comes from the fact that there are many participants in the system, who are incentivized to keep their coins having value, and when there is a transaction, it is broadcast out to the network. Everyone who wants can have a copy of the ledger and verify it for themselves.

The way a new transaction happens is that it is broadcast, and then the transactions are grouped, and all of the "miners" look to incorporate these transactions but then also simultaneously need to solve a very computationally expensive math problem, and once they do, they create the new block and earn some coins. This is the setup of how the Bitcoin network works. There is a lot more technicality, but those are the basics.

A **block** is a group of transactions, and it's called a **blockchain** because each block is added to the previous one creating a chain, making it increasingly harder to modify the history of the ledger.

Bitcoin

Bitcoin is the most popular and widely known cryptocurrency. Bitcoin is also open source software and a digital currency, and it was created by Satoshi Nakamoto in 2008 and released in 2009. Satoshi Nakamoto is a person or a group; it's not known, so it has a mythic status in the Bitcoin community. Here, I'll use Bitcoin to refer to the project or network and bitcoin to refer to the coins or tokens.

There are a few important things to know if you want to learn about Bitcoin.

Wallet

If you want to have your own bitcoin or cryptocurrency, you need a wallet. A **wallet** is like a bank account that stores your cryptocurrency. The difference between a cryptocurrency wallet and a bank account is that, if you have some fraud with your bank, your money is stolen, or you forget your password, the bank can help you out. With a cryptocurrency wallet, if it's stolen or you forget your password, it is gone, and that's it. You fully control your own coins, which has an added layer of risk.

Why would anyone want that? Well, in the US, with a stable currency, many people might not see the value of having a very volatile currency that doesn't have as many protections. But there are many countries and areas where there could be hyperinflation, currency could lose all its value, and this could provide another way. There is a whole philosophical underpinning to Bitcoin and cryptocurrency, but truly, there are conflicting philosophies, and many people project their own philosophy onto it. Whether that is more of a techno-progressivism, libertarianism or anti-government, financial tech, or globalization, there are lots of different lenses to view Bitcoin.

So, first you need a wallet.

Address

With your wallet, you also have an address. An **address** is like your bank account number. Here is what a Bitcoin address looks like:

1G1AaHTrh6MyvfdAs8ubpC6NchcESa6Uf8

This address is related to the public key of the wallet. So, essentially, all cryptocurrency is built on public and private key cryptography.

To protect your wallet, you may have a password or passphrase. A password or passphrase would be what allows you to get access to your wallet, like a bank account password.

Addresses and their balances are public, not private, since the ledger is public, and anyone can have a copy of it. So, Bitcoin is not anonymous; it is pseudonymous. The information is public, but it's not linked to your identity directly.

Seed Phrase

Then, you also might have a private key or **seed phrase**. So, what does that mean? Well, if someone owns the wallet, they own the coins in the wallet. The wallet has addresses. The addresses are just public and private key pairs. The public address anyone can know. But the private key—this is really the secret password. If you have the private key, you own the coins. So, you should not share the private key. Often, the private key can look like a very long sequence of characters. Sometimes, to generate these private keys, this is done using seed phrases. These are usually twelve-word phrases, which then let you generate the private key. In this instance here, this twelve-word seed phrase is the private key and is the money. So, if you lose those or someone else gets access, they get your cryptocurrency.

Risks of Online Storage

There are also pitfalls with storage. If you store it in an online exchange and online wallet, those can get hacked. In exploring cryptocurrencies a while ago, I got a lot of Dogecoin, which is a cryptocurrency based on an internet dog meme. I had stored the Dogecoin in an online wallet, which got hacked, and the hacker drained the wallets. So, I lost all that money. This was an early way to learn the lesson; if you aren't controlling the private keys, it isn't your cryptocurrency, and if you store something in an online exchange, it can get hacked.

Many exchanges have been hacked, and there isn't any recovering the value like in a bank. Mt. Gox was one of the first Bitcoin exchange hacks, and $450 million of bitcoin was lost.

Prices

But despite all this, there remains increasing interest. That's because this is a new and powerful technology with a big promise and big idea—an open global money system that anyone can use and nobody can own. The hope is to bring down the cost of payments. But people also view Bitcoin as digital gold. Or as a speculative commodity. Or in a lot of different ways. So, it exists in this middle space. In 2010, one bitcoin was worth three-tenths of a cent. In 2011, it was worth $1. Then, in 2013, it reached $1,000. In 2017, the price of bitcoin got up to almost $20,000. Then it dropped to $3,000 and back to $10,000, then increased again to almost $20,000 in 2020.

The following page has a table with some of the bitcoin prices by year.

Buying, Storing, Sending

So, should you get any bitcoin? That is totally up to you, but you should be fully aware of the risks, which is it can get lost and hacked in all the ways I've explained in this book and more. SIM swap attacks are a particularly bad attack on cryptocurrency.

	Monthly Average	High	Low
2009	$0.00	$0.00	$0.00
2010	$0.18	$0.50	$0.00
2011	$5.68	$31.90	$0.30
2012	$8.45	$15.40	$3.90
2013	$260.35	$1,241.90	$13.20
2014	$513.04	$1,093.40	$91.70
2015	$276.23	$492.80	$157.30
2016	$589.80	$982.60	$350.40
2017	$4,299.76	$19,870.60	$739.50
2018	$7,183.13	$17,252.80	$3,177.00
2019	$7,325.84	$13,929.80	$3,368.20
2020	$11,499.10	$19,897.40	$3,869.50

Source: Investing.com, December 2020

How can you get cryptocurrency? Well, there are some things you can do where you can earn it, and people will pay you in it. Otherwise, you need to get it at some sort of exchange where you pay fiat (like US dollars) and get bitcoins. A popular exchange for this is Coinbase, which I have used. Note: this is a custodial wallet; they are the ones who own your private keys, not you, and if they get hacked, you lose your cryptocurrency.

If you want a noncustodial wallet, that is one where you own and are responsible for your private keys and passwords. These could be mobile wallets.

If you want to store cryptocurrency, you can store them in an exchange (least secure and not recommended) or in a wallet (and that wallet can be online or offline). An offline wallet means it is not connected to the internet all the time. There is another layer of security, which is a **hardware wallet**. These are actual physical devices that store your cryptocurrency keys; a few that are more popular are Trezor and Ledger. There's an irony here, which is that for the most digital online currency, the most secure way of storing it is totally offline. Since the money is actually the private key, and the private key could be represented by a password, then actually, the money is just the information. Just like the bits we talked about earlier.

This means you can visualize some James Bond-type scenario where someone is transporting huge amounts of money across borders, but they don't carry anything; they just memorize the twelve-word seed phrase of the private key in their head...think about it.

Some people may take their passphrase or private key and write it on paper. Or...put it in a bank. Or on some other file or place you store backups. But this is up to you, and this does show the complexity of backing up cryptocurrency. This is an area where you can clearly see the tradeoff between security and convenience. A good middle ground today, I think, is using mobile noncustodial wallets, meaning you fully control it. Then, you back up your password in several places.

Ethereum

Bitcoin is currently the most well-known and most valuable cryptocurrency. The second most valuable cryptocurrency is **Ethereum**. There are lots of others, and sometimes people refer to anything that isn't bitcoin as an **altcoin**. Many of these cryptocurrencies have different approaches, but some often start with the same codebase and are **forks**, meaning they copy and start their own version.

So, what is the difference between Bitcoin and Ethereum or any of the others? There's a bit of a confusing difference in talking about Ethereum and Bitcoin. Bitcoin can refer to the project, the cryptocurrency, and the token. With Ethereum, it is the project, the cryptocurrency, but the actual token is called **ether**. In Bitcoin, there is a hard maximum of 21 million bitcoins, and in Ethereum, there is not a hard cap.

However, to understand the differences between Bitcoin and Ethereum, you want to take a bigger step back. **Ethereum** is well known for handling smart contracts or being more programmable than Bitcoin. Bitcoin has a much more limited scripting language, while Ethereum is Turing complete, meaning it could program anything.

So, Ethereum can even be thought of as a huge distributed global computer. Applications that run on Ethereum or other related types of blockchain platforms are called **dApps**, or **distributed applications**. People like to ascribe all sorts of things to their favorite projects, but even though cryptocurrency has been around for a decade, it's still relatively experimental.

People look at Bitcoin as something like "digital gold," a store of value, a currency, and a commodity.

With the programmable components of Ethereum, the use cases around it are slightly different.

Smart Contracts

One important part of Ethereum to understand is **smart contracts**. These are written in a language like Solidity (which is like C or JavaScript) or a few other languages. These contracts are just programs, just code, and they are actually run or executed on the Ethereum blockchain.

Today, there are still lots of usability issues with smart contracts; they could be hard to modify, and bugs could result in difficult-to-change errors. There was a security issue with Ethereum in 2016 that led to a takeover of $50 million with the DAO, which even led to a split in Ethereum, or a fork. There are now two versions: the main version, Ethereum (ETH), and the other version, now called Ethereum Classic (ETC).

So, smart contracts have lots of tradeoffs. There are also lots of interesting applications. One that gained in popularity was the ability to create new tokens, or new cryptocurrencies, on top of the Ethereum blockchain. The standard for this is called **ERC-20**, which just specifies what functions are required in the smart contract (the program defining the new token).

The development of new tokens on Ethereum led to the use case of people raising money or doing crowdfunding on Ethereum. People would contribute money in the form of ether and get back new types of tokens. The logic of the contract encodes what will happen. Here, it could be:

```
If the contract receives ether
    Compute the exchange rate of ether to
       the new token
    Then send new tokens to the sender
```

What other uses might there be for smart contracts? There are a number already out there, lots that people are experimenting with, and I'm sure people will come up with more in the future. Right now, for various financial transactions that are facilitated by existing groups, people are building ways to do that on Ethereum. This means that the actual legal logic or logic in a proprietary system can be built into an Ethereum smart contract that anyone can see. With Ethereum and distributed applications, people are building lending sites, exchanges, and investing tools based on smart contracts.

Smart contracts are also really digital contracts; it's something where the logic for the contract is written as a computer program, not just as a legal document.

Smart contracts could be used in financial applications, like options, insurance, or even exchanges. Many of these use cases are experimental, but there will be ways to move things that were just in legal documents to computer programs. A legal document has many elements similar to code, but it's interpreted by humans, not computers.

Public Key Cryptography

A foundational building block of cryptography is public key cryptography. In **public key cryptography**, there are two sets of keys. The public key can be shared and known by others, and the private key is kept secret. These two keys are related and generated based on certain cryptographic algorithms.

Public key cryptography is the basis for TLS, which is the basis for HTTPS.

If you are trying to browse a website securely, send payment information, or send an encrypted message, these all use public key cryptography.

Specifically, a few of the ways this works are:

- **Public key encryption.** In public key encryption, the message is encrypted with the recipient's public key. This means only the recipient can decode it using their private key.

- **Digital signatures.** With digital signatures, you can verify authenticity. You sign a message with your private key, and it can be verified as authenticated using your public key.

This also becomes the basis for generating cryptocurrency wallets and addresses, which have combinations of public and private keys.

Diffie-Hellman Key Agreement

A famous algorithm that enables encrypted communication is the **Diffie-Hellman key agreement**.

The way this works is it allows two parties to set up a secure communication secret over a public network.

One way to understand the math behind it is to understand how this might work using different paint colors. Note: this is complicated, so it may take a few times reading it to understand.

In cryptography, many of the examples are with Alice and Bob, characters easily represented by the letters A and B in diagrams. Here is the process:

- Alice and Bob agree publicly on a common paint color.
- Alice and Bob each pick their own secret paint color.
- Now they mix each of their secret paint colors with the common paint color.
- Now they can send each other the mixed paint color.

Alice

Bob

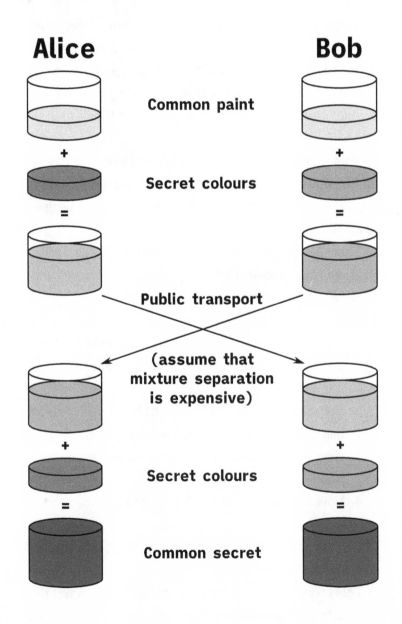

Common paint

Secret colours

Public transport

(assume that mixture separation is expensive)

Secret colours

Common secret

Then, each of them can mix their own secret paint color with the mixture they just received. Now, at this point, they have a new paint color (or secret) that any outside observer can't know. The security basis of this is that "unmixing" paint colors is a very difficult process to do.

This is actually done with math—and prime numbers, and modulus arithmetic—but the step-by-step process is the same. Now they have a shared secret that can be used as an encryption key.

There's another nice way to understand the Diffie-Hellman key agreement with locked boxes.

Here are the steps:

1. Alice puts a secret message in a box, locks it with a padlock that only she has the key to open and sends it to Bob
2. Bob adds a second padlock to the box, which only he has the key to open, and sends it back to Alice
3. Now Alice removes her lock and ships the box back to Bob
4. Now Bob removes the lock and can open the secret

The box always has one lock on it while it is in transit, so it can't be intercepted.

This is one you could even try out! And it gives you the basic idea behind establishing a secret key for encryption.

Alice   Bob

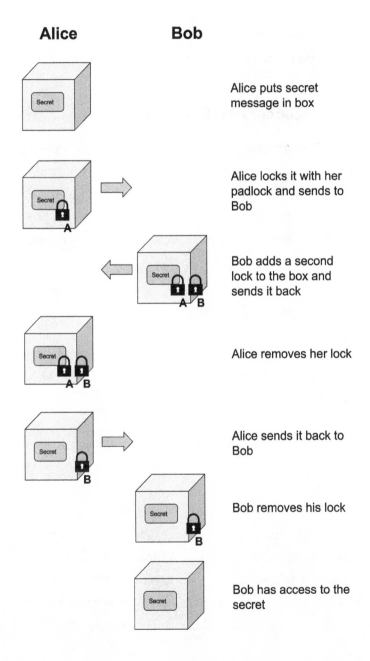

Alice puts secret message in box

Alice locks it with her padlock and sends to Bob

Bob adds a second lock to the box and sends it back

Alice removes her lock

Alice sends it back to Bob

Bob removes his lock

Bob has access to the secret

This step-by-step process of the Diffie-Hellman key agreement is an algorithm. The world of code is full of those.

A Cryptocurrency Phishing Scam

In the digital world, you have to stay alert, and cyberse-curity basics can help you do that. On July 15, 2020, many high-profile Twitter accounts, including Elon Musk, Bill Gates, Barack Obama, Joe Biden, Kanye West, and more, were taken over to promote a Bitcoin scam. Here is a sample of what one tweet said:

> I am giving back to the community.
>
> All Bitcoin sent to the address below will be sent back, doubled! If you send $1,000, I will send back $2,000. Only doing this for 30 minutes.
>
> bc1qxy2kgdygjrsqtzq2n0yrf2493p83kkfjhx0wlh
>
> Enjoy!

Now, with your new knowledge, we better understand what happened. A hacker used a targeted phishing attack, or social engineering, to gain access to Twitter admin-istrative tools, which allowed the hacker to send mes-sages posing as influential users. The message has a few suspicious features, including a sense of urgency and a request for money. They requested Bitcoin, so that the transaction could not be reversed, and shared a Bitcoin address to receive the money.

7
Algorithms

100101010101101000101010100010101010101000101010101010101010101010111010101100101010100101010101010101010101010010101

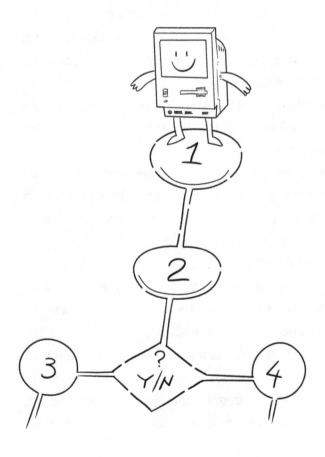

In high school, I took my first computer science class. When you make a breakthrough in learning to code, there is an *aha* moment. The *aha* moment is when you realize, *Wow, this is powerful stuff.* Or you make something work after tinkering around, and you can say, "I did that!" One of the first programs I wrote where I had the *aha* moment was writing a guessing game. It's a simple program, but it's cool! The idea is to write a program where the user chooses a random number, and then the computer tries to guess it, and you give clues to guess higher or lower. I'll share the algorithm for a guessing game in this chapter.

An **algorithm** is just a step-by-step process that the computer will follow. You can develop an algorithm to play a guessing game.

There are many other places we see step-by-step processes. What's your morning routine? Wake up, brush your teeth, shower, make your bed, have breakfast—some variation of that. Whatever your routine is, it's a step-by-step process. It's an algorithm.

What's your favorite thing to bake? I enjoy making cookies. You need to preheat the oven; then, you need to get the eggs, flour, and sugar and combine ingredients in a specific way. This recipe is a step-by-step process. It's an algorithm.

When you write a program that will have Karel the Dog put a tennis ball in every location of the world, you need to come up with a specific, step-by-step process to do this. You might go row by row, filling up each row and then zig-zagging up. Or go down a row, then double back and go up, and keep doing that until the end. Either way, this defines an algorithm. Specifically, once you've turned that algorithm into pseudocode and, later, a well-defined program, then it's something the computer can do.

But you can think about algorithms much more broadly to understand them.

Let's revisit my morning-routine example; this might be your algorithm:

Morning Routine Algorithm
```
Wake up
Brush teeth
Shower
Make bed
Have breakfast
```

It's a clear set of step-by-step instructions. When you are doing this for a computer, however, you need to be very specific. Does the computer already understand what it means to "Make bed," or do you need to define that more specifically?

So, what's an algorithm?

An algorithm is a sequence of instructions we give to computers to solve a particular process.

An algorithm also might be a solution to a problem. And while some algorithms are complicated, they don't need to be.

Search Algorithms

Say you have a deck of cards, and you want to find a particular card, say the nine of spades. How would you find it? You could say, "Well, you just look for it." But to make this an algorithm, you need to define it specifically, in a way that can be done repeatedly. Say your deck is all shuffled up. Here is a possible algorithm:

```
Find Card Algorithm
Start at the top of the deck
For every card in the deck
   Look at the card
   If it is the card I am looking for, I'm done
   Otherwise, move to the next card
```

Now that is very specifically how you might find a card in an unsorted deck of cards. There is a whole list of search algorithms since searching happens to be a problem that comes up in computer science all the time.

How might you find a definition for a word in the dictionary? (Say a real, physical dictionary book.) One way would be to start at the beginning and go page by page until you find it. That would look a lot like our find card algorithm.

Find Word in Dictionary Algorithm
```
Start at the beginning of the dictionary
For every word in the book
   Look at the word
   If it is the word I am looking for
      Get the definition, and I'm done
   Otherwise, keep going
```

The problem here is this could take...a long time. What if the word starts with Z? Or even M? You could try to make this a little easier by jumping to the letter of the alphabet first. Let's see how that might change the algorithm.

Find Word in Dictionary Algorithm 2.0
```
Get the first letter of the word you are
      looking for
Jump to the section of the dictionary for
      that letter
For every word in the dictionary starting
      with that letter
   Look at the word
   If it is the word I am looking for
      Get the definition, and I'm done
   Otherwise, keep going
```

This way could potentially save us a lot of time. There's a whole world of algorithmic analysis, understanding algorithmic complexity, which looks at how fast an algorithm might be and how it performs under different conditions.

Now we are going to play a game. The game is a guessing game. Pick a number 1–100. Got it? Okay, now I'm going to guess it.

Is it 1? Is it 2? Is it 3? Is it 4? Is it 5? Is it 6?...

You see where this is going. I'll let you in on my algorithm, which isn't that good yet.

Guess Number Algorithm 1.0
```
Start at 1
Keep repeating until I guess it right:
    Guess the current number
    If I'm right, I'm done
    Otherwise, increase my guess by one
```

If the number you guessed was 99, that would take me a long time. On average, it would take me about 50 guesses. So, not great. Imagine if that list was even longer or even had a million numbers.

Can you come up with a better way to guess the number? One thing you might do is start in the middle. Say you picked the number 40. Here's a different approach I could try:

Is it 50? No, lower.

Is it 25? No, higher.

Is it 37? No, higher.

Is it 43? No, lower.

Is it 40? Yes.

In my algorithm of starting at one and guessing one higher each time, I only eliminated one option. Here, I guess in the middle, find out if it's higher or lower, and eliminate half of the remaining options.

Here is my algorithm:

```
Guess Number Algorithm 2.0
The bottom of my range is 1
The top of my range is 100
Keep guessing until I get it right
   Calculate the middle of the range
   Guess current number
   If it's right, I'm done
   If it's higher
      The bottom of my range is one higher
         than my guess
   If it's lower
      The top of my range is now one lower
         than my guess
```

That's the algorithm I just used to guess your number, which is called **binary search**. And it will work pretty well even if our number is very big.

How many guesses will it take to guess a number 1–100? Seven guesses.

How many guesses will it take to guess a number 1–1,000? Ten guesses.

What about 1 to 1 million? Only twenty guesses. Pretty crazy. If we tried our initial version, guessing one at a time, in order, that would take 500,000 guesses on average. You can start to see the power of coming up with a good algorithm.

Test an Algorithm

Visit the example code for this chapter at *readwritecodebook.com*, and you can try playing the guessing game program with the algorithm described in this chapter.

Shortest Path

You pick up a paper map. (Do you have a paper map?) You're at home, and you are trying to plan a route to go to your friend's house. You can scan the map, look at which direction it is, and try to connect a path there. Say you are planning a road trip, and there are a few more options for getting from point A to point B. How might you actually do that? Today, I might use Google Maps. Plug in a destination, and it calculates potential routes. While I don't know what algorithm Google Maps uses, there are some foundational algorithms in computer science that are related to this type of planning.

A famous algorithm to know is **Dijkstra's algorithm**, or the **shortest path algorithm**. This algorithm helps us find the shortest path between two points. The question might be, "How do you get from a map or roads out in the world to a version of this that a computer can understand?" In code, we represent it using **graphs**—graphs here are not like the kind where you are plotting a line on an x- and y-axis. Here, a graph represents a collection of **nodes** and **edges**.

A graph you might be familiar with is the "social graph" popularized by Facebook and other social media companies. Each node on the graph is a person. Each edge on the graph is a line connecting two people, which represents that they are friends.

Here is an image that represents a small graph of friends. Each circle is a "node" that represents a person. Each line is an "edge" that represents a 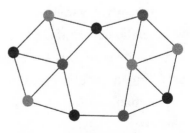 connection on the network, meaning they are friends with each other.

Let's look at another graph. Here is a graph which represents a simple map of US cities.

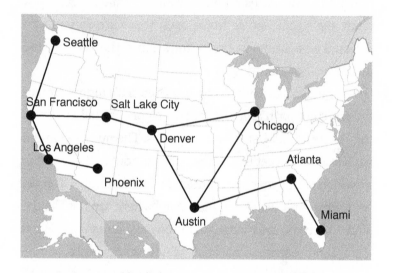

To understand this map as a graph: the nodes are the cities, which are the circles, and the edges are the roads or highways, which here, are just the lines between the cities.

Now, say we want to get from San Francisco to Chicago; what is the best route to take? You can abstract this map into the idea of nodes and edges, and at that point, we can apply any algorithm that works on graphs. This is a simplified map, but the principles still apply to a more complex map.

With this background, we can now come back to the road trip planning question. What is the shortest way to get from San Francisco to Chicago? You could just pick randomly and start guessing. That actually could be an algorithm, maybe not a very good one, though.

Dijkstra's algorithm is one that helps us find the shortest path. The way it works is we take all the cities and those become the nodes, and all the roads become the edges.

Here are the steps:

First, there is the "source," which is the place in the map (here, the "graph") we are starting. The source is going to be San Francisco. The source is the starting point.

Then, there is the "target," which is the place we are going, or the destination. Here, that is Chicago.

We're going to start with the source and then go to every other city and label it by saying it has an unknown distance from the source.

Next, we'll put them all into a list, where we can take out the best option first (called a **priority queue**). So, we take out the best option first. This will be our source (since it starts with 0). Then, we go to all the neighboring cities, ones we can get to directly from San Francisco.

This would be all the cities connected to San Francisco on our graph; here, this would be Seattle, Salt Lake City, and Los Angeles.

Then, we add the current distance (0) to the distance to that city. If that option was better than our previous way of getting to the city, we save that value. Then, we keep doing that.

How can that work? One way to see this is to step through an algorithm and see how it works. Follow what happens at each step, write it down, and visualize it.

Another place where you might see the idea of shortest path in a graph pop up is on the site LinkedIn. LinkedIn is a site for professional social networking. LinkedIn might tell you if you are connected to someone and how closely you are connected if you aren't yet connected. So, they may say you have a second-degree connection or a third-degree connection.

A second-degree connection would be that you share a mutual connection.

Third degree would mean you are connected by a connection's connection. To find this out, you could find the shortest path between you and another contact on LinkedIn using Dijkstra's algorithm.

Recursion

You could think of algorithms as functions; they may have an input and output and define a process. In the course of writing your algorithm, you'll use various commands and instructions to solve the problem. Say we are writing our card deck searching algorithm, we might use **for** loops and test out results with conditional statements.

In certain algorithms you write, you'll write a function that calls itself. This is called **recursion**. It's a bit of a confusing and mind-warping concept, so here are a few ways to think about it.

A way to see a recursive function and algorithm would be to compute the Fibonacci numbers. The Fibonacci numbers are defined like this:

The initial number, Fibonacci(0), is 0.
The next number, Fibonacci(1), is 1.
Then, every Fibonacci number after that is the sum of the previous two.

This means:

$$\text{Fibonacci}(n) = \text{Fibonacci}(n - 1) + \text{Fibonacci}(n - 2)$$

So, the next Fibonacci number is Fibonacci(2) = 0 + 1 = 1.
Here's the first several Fibonacci numbers:

0, 1, 1, 2, 3, 5, 8, 13, 21, 34

You can see each one is the sum of the previous two. When something is "defined" in terms of itself, this is recursive.

In recursion, you'll have the **base case**, which is something you will predefine. Here, the base case is the first two Fibonacci numbers, predefined as 0 and 1.

Here's what the code for computing Fibonacci numbers would be in Python:

```
# This is a recursive Fibonacci function
def fibonacci(n):
  # This is the base case
  if n == 0:
    return 0
  if n == 1:
    return 1

  # This is the recursive case
  return fibonacci(n - 1) + fibonacci(n - 2)
```

Notice that the last line of the function actually calls the function itself! The **fibonacci** function calls the **fibonacci** function. That is what makes it recursive. The first few lines of the function are the base cases. If we didn't have that, the function would go on forever, until you killed the program, which would be called infinite recursion.

```
# This prints the first 10 fibonacci numbers
for x in range(10):
  print(fibonacci(x))
```

To get a sense of a few more recursive functions, here is a recursive function that computes exponents.

Say we want to compute x^y power, like 2^3 power. What would that be? One way to think of it is that it's 2^2 × 2 again. So, to solve a recursive problem, you always make it one step smaller. This uses inductive reasoning: the idea is that if you solve it for the base case, and then you solve it for the "nth" case, this means you've solved every case. This is a really powerful idea! It can take a while to sink in.

The base case with exponents is that a number to the power of zero, like 2^0, equals 1.

Here's our approach written as pseudocode. You'll notice I'll write it out in pseudocode first because it's often an easier way to understand the algorithm, and then you can write it in a programming language. Also, the pseudocode is not specific to a programming language, and you could implement it in many different languages.

```
Recursive Exponents
Power(m, n)
Base case:
   If our exponent n is 0, then return 1
Recursive case:
   Return the result of Power(m, n-1)
        multiplied by m again
```

As Python code, this would look like:

```python
# Recursive function for exponents
# computing m to the nth power
def power(m, n):
```

```
if n == 0:
    return 1
return power(m, n - 1) * m

# Test this out on power of 2
for x in range(10):
    print(power(2, x))
```

TRY IT

Recursive Exponents

You can see the code and try running this program for yourself in the examples section for this chapter at *readwritecodebook.com*. This prints powers of 2. Can you modify it to print powers of 3?

A visual example of recursion is the Russian Matry-oshka dolls. These are dolls which are one inside the other, increasingly of smaller size. To solve one problem, you make it just a bit smaller and smaller and smaller and smaller until you reach the base case, the smallest doll in the set, which itself doesn't open.

Backtracking

There are lots of other algorithms and techniques, but here's one more that is fun to know. This algorithm is called **backtracking**, which can often be implemented recursively. What backtracking does is start to try and solve a problem by going forward, but if it runs into a step that can't work, it stops and goes backwards, returning to a previously valid step.

This could help us solve a maze or solve a sudoku puzzle.

Imagine you are going into a maze. A technique you might use is to walk down one path until you hit a dead end and then "backtrack" until you have another way to try. You probably already do something like that! The challenge here is taking an idea you have, or a process, and then turning that into something very specific that a computer can understand.

Here is the general pseudocode for a backtracking algorithm. Here, we are going to call the current location "currentState."

```
Backtracking Algorithm
FUNCTION Backtrack(currentState)
# Our base case is the current state is
# invalid or the problem is solved
IF  invalidState(currentState)
  THEN  return
```

```
IF  isSolutionState(currentState)
   THEN  we've reached our answer
# Next, try every possible next state from
# this current one and call Backtrack on it
REPEAT for every next place I can go from here
   Backtrack(nextState)
```

So, our pseudocode looks a little more advanced now. But let's try and manipulate it a bit, so it looks like a maze, or at least uses the language of a maze.

```
FUNCTION SolveMaze(currentState)
# Check if you are at a valid maze location
# which would be one that is in the maze
# and not yet visited
IF  invalidState(currentState)
   then return false

# Check if you made it to the end
IF  isSolutionState(currentState)
   then return true

# Try going north, east, south, and west
Mark that I've visited this location
   IF SolveMaze(north) return true
IF SolveMaze(east) return true
IF SolveMaze(south) return true
```

```
IF SolveMaze(west) return true
Unmark that I've visited this location
return false
```

TRY IT

Solve a Maze with a Backtracking Algorithm

You can see this algorithm in action to solve different mazes. Visit this example at *readwritecodebook.com* and then watch how it solves a maze by exploring various pathways, marking locations as it goes, and backtracking when it hits a dead end.

Solve a Maze with Karel

With algorithms and coding in general, there are usually many ways to solve a problem. Once you have an algorithm or a program, you can then look at the tradeoffs. Sometimes, there are nice, simple algorithms to solve a unique puzzle. Let's take our maze-solving question from earlier and bring back our favorite computerized dog, Karel.

Say we wanted to have Karel solve a maze? How could we do that?

One famous maze-solving algorithm is known as the right-hand rule, which works on mazes where the walls are all connected. The right-hand rule is where you put your right hand on the wall of the maze and keep walking forward, always keeping your hand on the wall. If you keep doing this, you'll reach the exit.

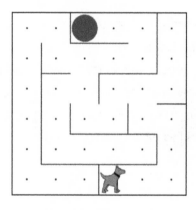

Here's the code for Karel to solve a maze using the right-hand rule:

```
/*
Karel uses the right-hand rule to solve the
maze. The end of the maze has a ball, and
Karel ends facing east.
*/
```

```
while(noBallsPresent()){
  if(rightIsClear()){
    turnRight();
  }
  while(frontIsBlocked()){
    turnLeft();
  }
    move();
}
takeBall();
faceEast();

/* Turn Karel to face east. */
function faceEast(){
  while (notFacingEast()){
    turnRight();
  }
}
```

You can watch Karel solve a maze and step through all the commands on the example on the site at *readwritecode book.com.*

Whether you are guessing a number, solving a maze, or even trying to make a prediction, algorithms are the next step in solving problems with code.

8
Artificial Intelligence

100101010101010010101010100101010010010101010101010101110101011010101001010101010010010010101001010101

I'm on a trip in China, and I'm walking around the water-front area in Shanghai known as the Bund. The signposts for crossing the street are a bit different there. In the US, there is usually a blinking light on the corner telling you to stop or to walk. There were blinking lights on the road, and there was a pole on the other side of the street. On that pole was a screen showing a surveillance video of the people crossing that particular street. As I walked across, it zoomed in on a particular person's face. I felt confused and alarmed as I tried to understand what was happening.

It seems this was identifying someone who may have been jaywalking. China has advanced surveillance and facial recognition so somehow identified a face of a partic-ular person to highlight. How does this work? What does it mean for a computer to learn something like this?

What Is Artificial Intelligence?

Facial recognition is one thing computers have "learned" to do. Facial recognition is just code, just an app, or just a program like any other program. However, it would fall under the category of artificial intelligence. **Artificial intelligence** (sometimes shortened to **AI**) is when com-puters simulate things that we normally associate with human intelligence. Some of the main categories are reasoning, planning, learning, natural language, and perception.

It might be easier to understand with some examples.

Under the perception category would be things like computer vision. Can a computer see? Well, not really in the way you see, but people are creating programs that try to achieve a similar result. A computer gets some image, some pixels, and then needs to figure out what it is. So, areas that fall under this category could be something like facial recognition, training a computer to recognize particular faces. While this is really easy for humans to do, it's quite complicated to get a computer to do it. It could be getting a computer to recognize an object. For example, say you have a picture of your desk, can it identify what is on your desk? This could also be speech recognition. Say you said something to your phone with Google or Siri; how does it know what you are saying?

Within the natural language processing category is figuring out how computers can understand human language. Artificial intelligence was my focus area in my computer science major in college, and what I find interesting about it is seeing that things that could be so easy for people can be so complicated for computers. With **natural language processing (NLP)**, we are trying to write programs that can understand the meaning of a sentence, answer questions about text, map the syntax of sentences, and translate between languages.

Lots of these artificial intelligence categories are now more readily accessible to people in the format of audio assistants like Alexa from Amazon, Google Assistant, and Siri from Apple.

Within the planning category are lots of problems related to robotics. One area is motion planning. How do you get a robotic arm to move to be useful in a factory assembly line? How could you move a robotic arm to complete a basic task? Again, this irony shows up in robot motion planning; lots of simple motions for humans are really hard for robots.

This is called Moravec's paradox, and it indicates that things that a child can easily do or are low level in humans can be challenging to teach computers. Completing simple movements like running or jumping, or understanding language is easy for children but hard for computers.

Within the learning category is teaching a computer how to do something, either from direct practice or indirectly. You may try to learn about correlations in data. Or learn to recommend particular movies. Lots of AI has been applied to game playing—how can you make a computer learn to play chess, or checkers, or Go?

And what does it even mean for a computer to "learn" something?

Machine Learning

What is machine learning? **Machine learning** is a part of artificial intelligence. Machine learning is figuring out how a computer can learn something and how you can teach it something. There are a number of techniques and categories.

In general, you first think about the task you are trying to solve or problem you are trying to learn about. Then, you can give the computer examples of different data. Then, the computer program creates a mathematical and statistical model to figure out what actions make sense based on the input data to get the best results.

The data that you give to the program to practice with is called the **training data**, or **training set**. Then, the computer creates a model of what to do.

One learning algorithm category is supervised learning. With supervised learning, the training data is labeled.

Step 1: Train the Model

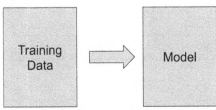

Step 2: Test the Model

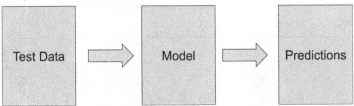

This means that we can see both the inputs and their results. Say we are trying to predict, or learn to guess, the price of a house based on the location and size. We might look at lots of examples of houses, locations, and sizes and get to see their prices. The prices are the results that we are then trying to predict. The locations and sizes, which are the columns in the data table, are considered the "features" of the model.

First, you create the model based on the training data. And then, you input test data to create your predictions.

Sample Training Data

ID	City	Size	Price
1	Chicago	1500	$400,000
2	Chicago	2000	$500,000
3	New York	1000	$800,000
4	Los Angeles	2000	$650,000
5	...	...	...

Test Process

ID	City	Size
100	Chicago	1700

Given an entry like this of a sample house, the algorithm would try to guess the price.

To run a test, you get a new entry that has city and size, and you need to guess the price. The model will output the guessed price.

Another category of machine learning algorithms is **unsupervised learning**. Here, our training data is not actually labeled with outputs. The algorithm is looking for the patterns in the data without the labels. An example of an unsupervised learning situation is when you want to find clusters in data, but your data may not be labeled beforehand. Say you were looking at a million tweets from Twitter and wanted to group them into categories; they aren't all labeled beforehand, so you could use unsupervised learning here.

Machine Learning Is Probability Plus Data

When you hear someone talk about AI or machine learning (ML) in the abstract, it sounds so futuristic or crazy. You hear it, and you might think, *How can that even work!?* But when you start to see the underlying mechanics, you can see how it might work.

Machine learning, or AI, is just code or a computer program. Oftentimes, people are using libraries with different algorithms that someone else has created. Remember, an algorithm is a step-by-step process to figure something out. With AI or ML, there is usually a question we are trying to answer or a problem we are trying to optimize.

Now, you have to figure out how you can turn your question into something a computer can understand.

You need to figure out your inputs, or features. And you need to figure out your outputs, or guesses, or labels.

Then, you take these pieces, and you use some sort of mathematical model—it's really a probabilistic model. You feed the algorithm some data, and then it tries to make the best guess.

Here are some examples of how you might break this down:

Task	Inputs	Labels	Data types	Guess
Facial recognition	Pictures of faces	Names	Pictures, pixels	Name
Object labeling	Pictures of objects	Names of each object	Pictures, pixels	Object name
Handwriting recognition	Pictures of handwritten letters and words	Actual letters or actual words	Pixels	Letter or word
Translate English to Spanish	English phrases	Corresponding Spanish phrases	Text, characters	Spanish phrases
Identify spam	Email messages	Spam or Not spam	Text, characters	Spam or Not spam

Once you've gathered your data and built your machine learning model or selected an algorithm and set up your program, you've really done most of the work. The computer doesn't really know this stuff like you do. But that's more of a philosophical question anyways—what does it mean for a computer to understand Spanish? But what it does have is a data set, and it creates probabilities. If it assigns a high probability to a translation, well, the higher the probability, the better the translation. And if the output is bad, sometimes feedback is given to the algorithm, either from a person or a computer, to make the guesses better in the future.

While this is a very complicated field that relies on a lot of intense math, it is possible to understand the basics. Artificial intelligence and machine learning are really probability plus data. You try to assemble a data set and then learn the patterns from the data set, which is just applying some sort of probabilistic model to the data and finding the optimization. Optimization means finding the parameters and values in your model that give the best predictions.

So, we've turned a question of human intelligence—who is that person?—into a question of crunching numbers and optimizing a function, which is something computers are really good at.

How Does a Spam Filter Work?

Task	Inputs	Labels	Data types	Guess
Identify spam	Email messages	Spam or Not spam	Text, characters	Spam or Not spam

If you use email, you know spam. **Spam** refers to junk mail, unsolicited mail, or lots of messages from the same website. To make your email more usable, the app will try to filter out spam messages, so you can just focus on the emails you want to be getting. It is estimated that 90 percent of emails that are sent is spam.

You may have a spam folder where you can see the messages your email application has identified as spam. While most spam filters are pretty good these days, they still get it wrong sometimes. Just yesterday, I realized an important email went to spam. This would be considered a false positive—it was labeled as spam (positive label), but it shouldn't have been. A false negative would be a spam message that makes it to your inbox (negative label) but should have been marked as spam.

A popular method for building a spam filter is based on an idea from probability theory called **Bayes Theorem** and which uses a **Naive Bayes Classifier**.

One of the first academic publications on Bayesian spam filters was written by a computer science professor of mine at Stanford, Mehran Sahami. It's a simple idea, but it is very powerful!

The way a Naive Bayes model works for identifying spam is that it looks at all the words that appear in an email. Some words are more likely to show up in a spam email, and some are less likely. In the training step, the model builds up probabilities that a word shows up in a spam email. The training data is made up of lots of emails, and those are identified and labeled as "Spam" or "Not spam."

Training Data

#	Email	Label
1	AMAZON.COM® COURTESTY CARD <amzn.2.gmsu.72723@6g7ijccru33q7q.w1.yj4znyy.cf> Welcome to Your Free $50 Amazon.com® Gift Card (HEADS UP: 24 Hours Left to Grab) **Dear Customer**, do you love online shopping at Amazon.com®... or hate it? Care to share your experience? Your opinion is worth $50 to us!	Spam
2	b08609044@ntu.edu.tw I have a business Proposal for you. please get back to me, it's very important...	Spam
3	yourfriend@gmail.com Question about homework Hi Jeremy- I had a question about the homework from yesterday.	Not spam
4	*Zippy Loan – Loan Manager* <zpln.2.gmsu.72381@wo7nco9cs4bbac.w2e22-1.oqjndtl.gq> **Need Funds? Get up to $15,000 FAST!** PERSONAL LOANS MADE SIMPLE AND FAST.	Spam
...	...	...

So, we collect the emails. We label them as "Spam" or "Not spam." This gives us the training data. These sample spam messages are actually snippets taken from my spam folder.

Some things we need to figure out are the answers to these questions:

- What is the probability a message is spam?
- What is the probability a message is not spam?
- What is the probability that any given word appears in a spam message?
- What is the probability that any given word appears in a non-spam message?

To do this, mainly, we just need to count the words. Take this sample email, ID #1:

Dear **Customer**, do you love online shopping at Amazon.com®... or hate it? Care to share your experience? Your opinion is worth $50 to us!

You are one of 5 customers selected to participate in our 30-second anonymous survey, today, May 22, 2020. 4 participants have already claimed their $50 reward. **What about you?**

Get Your Free

$50 Amazon.com®

Gift Card*

Hurry, your code AZ2020 expires in 24 hours!

Confirm your survey participation status here:

For example, we would track the number of spam emails that have the word "expires" and then the number of non-spam emails that have the word "expires." Say there are 10 emails—8 are spam; 2 are not spam. Say 4 of our 8 spam messages had the word "expires," and 0 of the 2 non-spam had the word "expires." Then the probability that this word shows up in a spam message is 4/8 or 50 percent.

We would track this using a dictionary or map to help us count. A dictionary lets us associate a key (the word) with the value (the number of times it appears in certain types of emails).

Here would be the pseudocode for a spam filter:

SpamFilter

```
Train Spam Filter
SpamWordCount = {}
NonSpamWordCount = {}
```

```
For every email
  For every word in the document
    If the email is spam
      Add count to SpamWordCount
    Else
      Add count to NonSpamWordCount
Compute probabilities
```

Testing Spam Filter
```
Compute probability of spam
Compute probability of non-spam
If spam score > non-spam score
  Return spam
Else
  Return not spam
```

There are many variations of this, and you may come up with special features as well, but just looking at the conditional probabilities of words can help you get started to see how you might create a spam filter.

Recommendation Systems

Let's look at another example: how does a recommendation system work? There are lots of ways! But how might you write a program that recommends movies or TV shows on Netflix, what else you could buy on Amazon, or other people you might follow on Twitter?

Could you figure out how you might apply an idea we've already seen to this? You could write a recommendation program using probability, counting, and Naive Bayes.

There are also lots of ways to do it. What is the magic sauce of Netflix's or Amazon's algorithms? They probably use all of the tons of data they have and advanced statistical or machine learning techniques. But you could simulate a basic one with ideas you know.

Here's how I might frame that question.

On Netflix, the question is:

What movies and TV shows should we recommend?

Or, stated alternatively:

Given that you have already watched and liked some movies and shows, what shows should we recommend?

How might you approach coding this up? Well, first, I can look at people who have watched similar shows as you. So, I can try to figure out how to create a similarity score or even just find people who watch shows that you watch.

Then, what shows do those people like?

You could, for every person who watches Netflix, make a list of the shows they like or the shows they watch.

Now it's time to recommend a show to you.

Say you like these shows: *Breaking Bad, Narcos,* and *House of Cards.* Now I will go find the people in our dataset who also like those three shows. So, say there are 1 million people who liked the three shows you like. Now, what other shows do most of those people like?

What I would do is create a dictionary, or a counter, or a map—some way to associate the popularity of a show within this group of users.

Say that within this group, we consider four other shows:

- *Sherlock*
- *Black Mirror*
- *Stranger Things*
- *Money Heist*

Out of this group of 1 million people, here are how many liked each show:

- *Sherlock:* 300,000
- *Black Mirror:* 700,000
- *Stranger Things:* 350,000
- *Money Heist:* 500,000

What show might you recommend? I would recommend *Black Mirror* because, out of people who liked the same shows you liked, this show was also the most popular among them. From a probability standpoint, we are picking the highest conditional probability.

So, the magic of recommending a TV show can be broken down into the problem of gathering and organizing the data, coming up with a step-by-step process, and maximizing or optimizing some question. Now, I'm not saying this is how Netflix does it. But I am saying this is a plausible algorithm—a plausible step-by-step process—to recommend a show. This is also an English version explanation of what a Naive Bayes algorithm does. Which is that it uses conditional probability. **Conditional probability** means the use of the word "given." Given that you liked these shows (*Breaking Bad*, *Narcos*, and *House of Cards*), what show has the highest probability that you would like it?

Say there are 180 million people on Netflix. Say 10 percent of people like *Sherlock*, and 5 percent of people like *Black Mirror*. We wouldn't necessarily assume you would prefer *Sherlock*. We are going to filter it, given that you like other shows. They can apply all sorts of other techniques and machine learning models here. In 2009, Netflix ran a contest called the Netflix Prize with a million-dollar grand prize for the best recommendation algorithm.

Netflix gave a training set with 100 million ratings that about 500,000 users gave to 18,000 movies. They were of the form:

```
<user, movie, date of grade, grade>
```

The participants had to write an algorithm to predict a grade, and the winner is whoever does best on the test set, where they don't see the ratings. Here's a summary of the problem.

Task	Inputs	Labels	Data types	Guess
Recommend movie	User, Movie, Date, Grades	Grade	Numbers, Dates	Grade

However, the important part here is thinking about how you might take an abstract problem and break it into something that you could actually solve, step by step, with a computer.

Are the Robots Taking Your Jobs?

You may have seen this in the news: the robots are coming for your jobs. Is it true? Well, first, it's good to understand what even is meant by this statement. Is it an actual, physical robot doing your job, like a robot in *The Jetsons*? That could be. It could be a robot in a factory building a car or even a robot cooking some food. But often, the "robots" taking your jobs refer to artificial intelligence more generally. It may be more accurate in this instance to say that people are worried about AI taking their jobs. And in lots of cases, that AI isn't a physical robot. It's really just a software program or an app. Say there was a process that humans did as their jobs, and now a computer can do it... that could be an instance where AI is taking someone's job. So, are the doomsday claims all they are hyped up to be?

It is hard to say. There are all sorts of wild predictions about the robots taking our jobs, and what percentage of jobs could be replaced by AI or software. It's really hard to know. What has been the case for a very long time is that technology does replace jobs. It often replaces jobs and ushers in new ones. The elevator operator is a job we used to have, and this was replaced by...people pushing their own buttons on the elevator. There used to be jobs for telephone switchboard operators, who would manually connect two calls, and now people just call each other on a cell phone. A toll booth collector was a job and still is a job in some places but, now, is mostly replaced by...a toll booth machine. Now these are a few jobs that seem a bit more dated.

But what is the likelihood of computers, software, and AI replacing other jobs? And, while in the past technological change replaced jobs and created new ones, is it different this time?

There are around 2 million Uber and Lyft drivers and 3.5 million truck drivers in the US. If full self-driving cars come to consumers, how will that affect these drivers? Could software take more factory jobs? Could it take more white-collar jobs? This is an open question and debate, but I think it helps to understand for yourself where this technology is at and how it is changing.

Now, the big question: is it different this time? In the past, when one job might have gone away, it was replaced by different jobs, and people adapted. If self-driving cars displace lots of taxi and truck drivers in such large numbers, what will happen then? Self-driving cars likely will create all-new sorts of opportunities and jobs, but will the order of magnitude be off? In many cases, software has allowed tech companies to operate with significantly fewer employees than may have been needed with older companies. WhatsApp, a popular global messaging app, was bought by Facebook for $19 billion in 2014 when it only had fifty-five employees but had 420 million monthly active users. In an earlier era, a company with such a high valuation likely would need thousands of employees.

I think it may be different this time, and it might not just be a hiccup like elevator operators losing a job. The reason I think this today is because, with the way that the economy is more information-driven, there are not as many reasonably paying jobs that don't require more education. This means that, in the past, while someone may have lost a job to a technological shift, you could get a job that didn't have too strong of an education requirement, and that job was enough to cover basic living expenses. I'm not sure that is the case today with the US economy. The labor flexibility is such that if someone is displaced as a taxi, Uber, or truck driver, what types of jobs will people move into? In retail, there are 29 million workers. If retail changes a lot, where significantly fewer retail employees are needed, where will these workers go? I don't think there is easy labor fluidity today, and I think the orders of magnitude are different because of the software. Some of these technologies are still early, but still promising enough that this is worth learning about and bringing into public policy considerations. Andrew Yang ran as a presidential candidate advocating for the idea of Universal Basic Income based on the hypothesis that the robots and AI are taking jobs, and this is a shift the US isn't ready for. This may take ten to twenty years to see if this was just another unfounded fear of technology and the future, or if it really was a shift that could cause massive displacement.

I'd say, either way, if you don't want your job to get automated away, there is a good skill to have. You'd rather be able to code the computers than have to listen to them.

General Intelligence

Some of the AI that we've talked about actually isn't so smart. It's a software program that does things that computers are good at, like counting, computing proba-bility, or maximizing a function. But there is an ongoing quest within the field of artificial intelligence to build machines that can achieve what is referred to as general intelligence.

Artificial General Intelligence (AGI) refers to com-puters being able to do any type of intellectual task that a person can. General intelligence is also known as strong AI (as opposed to weak AI, which is similar to some of the examples from earlier).

General AI is the stuff of science fiction, and maybe what you think of when you imagine artificial intelligence or futuristic robots. It's a computer that could plausibly do anything a human could do, but then it is also a com-puter, so it can do all those things a computer is good at but people aren't. That would be things like solving hard math problems, searching among billions of documents, or running algorithms at billions of operations a second. General intelligence is also hypothesized about across sci-ence fiction books and movies.

In the movie *Her*, the software assistant has general intelligence.

In movies like *The Terminator* and shows like *Westworld*, you can see various examples of what people think the world could be like with artificial general intelligence.

Now, there is an important research question that emerges, which is: How do you know? How do you know that when it's happened, that the computer is "intelligent?" Famous computer scientist Alan Turing proposed the question, "Can machines think?"

There is another question of if a computer with AI can have a mind. What would that mean? This gets into the philosophy and ethics of AI, but would a computer feel or have self-awareness or be conscious? What would that mean? Does it understand something in the way that a person does? Does the difference matter?

The Imitation Game, or The Turing Test

How might you test if a computer could think? Or if a computer could achieve a general task as well as a human could? **The Turing Test** is a challenge proposed by Alan Turing to understand if a computer had general intelligence comparable to a human. In a paper he wrote, he called it the Imitation Game (and there is now a movie with that name). There are a few versions of it.

In the general version, there are three participants: There is an interrogator who cannot see either of the other two participants. The first player is a person and the second is a computer, and the interrogator gets to ask questions to try to determine which is which.

In the original Imitation Game proposed in the paper, there are three players. One is the interrogator, one is a person, and one is a computer. But here, the interrogator is trying to guess the gender of the two players, and the question is if the computer can successfully imitate that part.

When I think of the Turing Test today, I think of people trying to determine if a computer can pass for a human; that's sort of the shorthand it has taken on since the original paper. But there are lots of other possible tests. Could a robot/AI complete a job? Or get a college degree? How might you design a test to determine if an AI had general intelligence?

People to Know

Alan Turing was an English mathematician, computer scientist, and cryptographer and is also considered the father of artificial intelligence. During World War II, he worked for the British code-breaking unit and devised a machine called the Enigma machine to help break codes. He also proposed a model for a theoretical machine on an infinite tape called a **Turing Machine**, which is a model for a general-purpose computer. If a language is **Turing complete**, it can solve any problem a Turing machine could (so if you remember back to cryptocurrency, Solidity is Turing complete, and Bitcoin script is not).

Superintelligence

So, there is your simplest AI, which is just a basic statistical model that takes in data and makes predictions. This could be predicting prices, or flight delays, or guessing if something is fraud.

Then, there are your more advanced models, but they still take in data and output guesses or actions.

Then, there is the quest for general intelligence, to see if computers could match humans in human-type tasks.

But what's after that? What if computers achieved that and could go beyond that? This is an idea called **superintelligence**, which is where computers are orders of magnitude better than humans at lots of various tasks.

Part of the idea is that with every step in technology, the tools get better, and the rate of progress accelerates. So, the tools and rate at which AI is improving today is far faster than twenty years ago, and it will improve even faster in the future. When you take this idea to its logical conclusion, that the speed of technological progress continues to increase at an exponential rate and causes major changes to civilization, this idea is called the singularity. So, let me note: this is a very far out idea, highly contentious and still very speculative. But I think it's helpful to know the universe of ideas that are out there in AI of where we are today and where it can go.

This is the version of events where computers become too powerful, or take over, or solve some strange optimization problem and cause harm to humans.

Part of the reasoning behind it goes like this: say the machines we have are okay today. But then they improve a bit, and then a lot, and get to the point where they would be considered AGI. The most cited AI authors estimate a 50 percent chance of AGI by 2050 and 90 percent by 2070. It could happen—but it could also never happen! But say computers reach AGI. They can now do things at the level of intelligence of humans, but probably also some tasks much faster. So, at this point, these machines can design even better machines, which can design even better machines...and this leads to the idea of the "intelligence explosion" proposed by mathematician I.J. Good.

Robot Takeover Today

AI, in some respects, is simpler than you think. It's using probability, it's using data, it's using code, to make a prediction or to optimize a function. So, the robot takeover maybe isn't what you imagine. Yes, there are physical robots being built, but that's not really where you may be interacting with AI most in your day to day life.

AI is coming to your day-to-day life in a less nefarious way but likely still very transformative.

What is AI? Again, AI does not have to be the Terminator

or a smart assistant impersonating a human, though it could be.

AI is how Netflix recommends what shows you might like or what Amazon suggests you buy. AI is how the Facebook newsfeed figures out what to show you, and your bank determines if a charge is credit card fraud.

Sometimes it doesn't take something "smart" or "AI" to have a displacement effect. Some stores are introducing ordering via an iPad-like kiosk. Is this AI? Really, it's just a normal software program, but that might be the wrong question. This software could replace how people order in many restaurants; you might find it in a McDonalds and in more places soon.

Another example of AI I like is self-driving cars or autonomous vehicles.

Self-Driving Cars

Many companies are developing self-driving cars, or cars that drive themselves. No human driver, no steering wheel needed, the car somehow sees the road, and the computer figures out how to get you where you want to go.

In some ways, this is the same as that first code you saw with Karel:

```
move();
turnLeft();
```

It's the same process, but a bit more advanced. The car needs to use sensors to build up its picture of the landscape and environment. It needs to figure out what is there, what obstacles are present, where the road is, and if it is safe to go. Just like Karel has a world and commands to navigate the world, a self-driving car is a more open-ended version of the same problem.

This combines lots of aspects of AI and machine learning, and even big data. Companies like Google are building self-driving cars through the company Waymo. Tesla is building self-driving cars with its autopilot technology.

So, how does a self-driving car work?

First, to build up the environment, it uses sensors. These are physical devices that map the world. The computer doesn't see the world like you do, but it needs to figure out where it is, with something like GPS. But it needs to know this very specifically, so it may use radar or lidar (with lasers) to come up with a much more detailed map.

It needs to identify people and stop signs and cars around it. Then, it could create its own map of the world.

Then, it needs to issue commands to the car. Again, this is just like Karel; we need to give those instructions. The car can move; it can speed up, slow down; it can turn left or turn right. At the same time, the code is monitoring it.

The actual ML/AI techniques used in self-driving cars can be very advanced. There are cars like this on the roads, and there are cars like this which are on the roads where there are actually humans training them. But even so, the technology has not yet hit prime time. It's still speculative if it will come to the general public sooner or later or not for a while. I think it will continue to develop and bring some big changes to driving in cities and urban design, but we will see as time goes on.

Issues to Know: Bias in Artificial Intelligence Algorithms

As AI develops, there are many ethical questions to wrangle with. One question to consider where you can already see the impacts today is the impact of the bias in artificial intelligence algorithms.

An algorithm is a step-by-step process, and it's something that is followed to get a result. Now, with our AI and ML models, the algorithm learns from the program that we wrote, the assumptions that are built-in, and also the training data, or training set.

The results that come from the algorithms aren't objectively correct but depend on all of these inputs.

Now, what happens if the inputs to the training data are biased? Say you are creating facial recognition software, but it is mostly tested on white faces. How does facial recognition work with people of other races? Some studies of facial recognition algorithms in the US have found that it may misidentify Black, Asian, and Native

American people ten to one hundred times more often than white people.

Now, lots of other use cases of AI might be predictive. You may look at crime data and try to analyze it—there is software like this biased against Black people—it's not an objective algorithm, it's an algorithm built with the assumptions of the people who built it, and those assumptions are embedded into the system. What kinds of problems should be solved? How should the AI be used? What factors should be considered in developing the AI? The AI programs are being built either way, but we should want varying approaches and perspectives with it.

What if a company could identify pregnant shoppers before they knew they were pregnant themselves? This is what happened at Target. The question to ask is, "How should this be approached?" What should be allowed, and what shouldn't be? Right now, algorithms and predictions are being developed for so many things. I saw one version of this firsthand in China as they had widespread facial recognition, and I think the use-case there is concerning. Many of the places using AI won't be visible, but it's being used behind the scenes.

Predictive algorithms with AI are going to be used to guess, determine, and make decisions. How should these be created? What are the risks and tradeoffs in the way they are built? These are some of the important questions for people to think about. And this is part of the reason we make learning about coding accessible to more people.

9
Computer Science Education

10010101011010001010101000101010010100101010101010101011101010110010101000101010101010101010010010101

My philosophy working in education has been that you have to go and get out there and actually see how things are going in the classroom. Earlier on, in CodeHS, I took two cross-country road trips to visit schools and run coding workshops for students. The first trip in 2013 was just in my car, and we wanted to visit anyone who would let us—we ran thirty-five workshops, visited forty-four states, and drove over 12,000 miles. I stayed in random motels, couch surfed, and sometimes stayed with friends if they lived in the area. The next time, in 2015, we got a van, wrapped it so that it was bright pink and had the CodeHS logo on it, then did sixty workshops and had CodeHS team members joining in different places along the way.

I've visited urban schools, rural schools, suburban schools, public schools, charter schools, and private schools. I've visited some very fancy schools and many under-resourced schools. I visited a lot of places where no one ever comes to visit their school.

I've visited hundreds of schools for computer science all around the country and now the world. The current state of CS education is highly varied, but there are noticeable trends I've seen. Throughout my time working in coding education, I've been excited to find ways to share that *aha* moment with students and teachers. You start with the thought, "Wouldn't it be cool if...?" and then see if you can make it happen. Creating with coding is about possibility.

How I Learned Coding

My journey in learning to code has been one combining both formal and informal learning. My first experience in coding was making a personal website with HTML and CSS when I was fourteen. I tried to figure this out on my own. I tried making a website for one of my classes and then, later, made a website for a comedy newspaper I started in high school. I took my first computer science class in high school in Java when I was sixteen. I was able to write some basic programs, do computations, and create a few interactive games, from a simple guessing game to a blackjack game. As I learned more, I was able to make the website for the comedy newspaper better, from being just an HTML page to using a tool called WordPress.

At college, I took a class in C++ programming and then a class on how to make iPhone apps. I created and managed a site for a comedy newspaper I started at Stanford. Since I was in an iPhone programming class, I built an iPhone app for the comedy newspaper too.

I took more classes later on in C and in computer science theory.

My sophomore year, I took classes in web development, human-computer interaction, and artificial intelligence and on teaching computer science. That was when I became a student teacher and starting teaching computer science.

I built lots of projects on the side for things I was interested in and involved in. I had an interest in puzzles, and we did puzzles for *The Flipside* (the comedy newspaper), so I built a tool to create jumble puzzles and cryptograms. I created a tool to allow us to do code commenting for the Stanford computer science classes when I was a TA to give students feedback. One summer after college, a few friends and I worked on making a site called Raunk, where you could create ratings and rankings, like for your favorite movies or favorite foods.

I took many more classes and built other projects as well. I tried to connect what I was learning to what I was interested in and find real-world ways to apply it. I am very lucky that I had an opportunity to try to learn it on my own, to take classes in high school and college, and to create projects. But I think we can give this opportunity to so many more people now as we create better tools to make learning to code easier to do.

Learning to code gave me the opportunity to start a company. In 2012, when we were seniors at Stanford, I started CodeHS with my friend and college roommate, Zach Galant. We had both been computer science majors and teaching assistants and had creative ideas of how to apply what we learned. We started CodeHS in a class and then continued working on it after graduating.

Why Learn Computer Science

You may be a student, or a teacher, or an educator more broadly, or an administrator. You may just be someone trying to orient yourself in the world of technology and coding. Why does this matter to you?

There are a few main reasons why this is so important in education. If you are a younger student, then this world of code and technology is one you are growing up in. You have the choice to just be a user and consumer of what is around you or to be an active creator of it. You can design it, build it, and make the choices that need to be made to build the important technology that people will use now and in the future.

It's a skill that applies across fields, no matter where you look.

You can follow coding in many directions for career opportunities, but that's not even the main reason. Even if your job doesn't directly involve coding, an understanding of this technology gives you tools to contribute across many areas.

If you are a teacher, this is the world that we are in today. You can let the technology pass you by, or you can also join along as a builder, tinkerer, and coder. You can create projects for your own classroom, you can explain and connect the dots for students, and you can have the confidence to teach this to students.

The world of coding, technology, and computing is too broad and vast for anyone to know all of it. I think it's helpful to have a broad sense of what's out there, and you can share that excitement with your students. But if you want to go deep in any area, from game design to machine learning, there is a whole world to discover.

And if you are responsible for larger education decisions, ask yourself What skills do you think are most important for students today? What is the direction that education is going? What is the direction that work is going? These are moving in the direction of technology, of code, of realizing it's a connected world and the issues and challenges to grapple with are still very complex. We need to proactively educate students on the basics, the fundamentals, give them the building blocks and creativity, and think about how they can be good stewards of the technology that will be built in the future.

K–12 Computer Science Education

Maybe now you are convinced and might want to learn more about coding and computer science. How does that all work? Where can you learn it for yourself? How are students learning today? What is the computer science education landscape like, and how is it changing?

Computer science education is still early. It looks different at different levels, from elementary to middle school to high school, college, and professional.

In K–12 education, there has been a big push recently to teach more coding in schools, but it's a topic that schools haven't fully been ready to teach. That's where we've been focusing at CodeHS, by working with schools and districts to implement computer science.

The goals and topics covered vary at different levels.

In elementary school, teaching coding is very exploratory. It's common to see games and puzzles and tablet apps. There are block-based coding platforms, including some like Scratch. Block-based coding allows younger students to create programs by dragging visual blocks to avoid having to type more complex syntax.

Later on, in middle school, the coding classes get more involved. In middle school currently, we see small coding units, semester coding classes, electives, and full-year coding classes. Sometimes, we see various pathways in middle school where students will have a chance to take a sequence of computer science courses that build upon each other.

At this point, middle school courses are still very introductory. These courses are often block-based courses, but depending on each student and school, sometimes students are starting to transition to text-based coding. Text-based coding would be using the full syntax of a language like Python or JavaScript.

Computer science courses in middle school are still very exploratory, teaching basic coding concepts. We have lots of popular courses that involve basic coding in a language like JavaScript or Python, web design, but also, we see that schools want to teach survey courses. In these courses, students will get to try out just a bit of programming or learn how computers or the internet works.

As it continues up to high school, the courses get slightly more standardized. There's a clear delineation in high school between the introductory and advanced computer science classes. In introductory classes, we similarly see lots of JavaScript, Python, Java, and web design. These are usually year-long classes but, sometimes, last for semesters. Most of the time, these will use text-based coding. Cybersecurity is also getting more popular as a course topic in high schools.

These introductory courses are the starting point—still, most schools don't have full computer science offerings, though many are responding to changing state standards.

Later on, it is more common to offer advanced courses. These could be AP Computer Science courses, like an AP Computer Science A course, which is a Java course that counts for college credit. There is also the newer AP Computer Science Principles course, which is a survey course on computer science topics but also a course for college credit. Additional advanced courses in high school we see are advanced versions of college-level intro courses, like web design, cybersecurity, or something like app development.

Diversity and Access to
Computer Science Education

As computer science becomes a more important and foundational skill, it's important that we make those classes and opportunities available to all students. Currently, access to computer science education in the US is very skewed. Less than half of K–12 schools offer computer science; if the schools don't offer it, the students won't be able to learn it. At the same time, nine out of ten parents want schools to offer computer science.

There are major gaps in access to computer science education for women and minority students, and this then plays out later in college, the workforce, and ultimately, the type of technology that gets built. If you look at AP Computer Science A exams as a measure of who has access to these courses, in 2018, only 4% of exams were taken by Black students, only 11% by Latino students, and only 0.16% by Native American students. Only 24% of exams were taken by female students. Black students and Latino students are also less likely to attend a school that offers computer science courses.

Out of those graduating with a bachelor's degree in computer science, only 17% are women, only 8% are Black, and only 9% are Hispanic. Only 25% of those working in computing-related fields are women, only 8.6% are Black, and only 6.8% are Latino.

We have to increase access to computer science education in schools, as this is the primary place students can take classes. This is a focus of ours at CodeHS: to enable schools and teachers to offer high-quality classes, and to offer training for teachers to run these classes. We've seen earlier the harmful impact that bias can have in algorithms and AI; bringing a more diverse group to create software will help mitigate that.

College Computer Science—What's in a CS major?

So, what is after computer science and coding in K–12? Well, one route to go is to study computer science in college. I took my first computer science class in high school; I took the AP Computer Science AB course in Java. I remember it being a fun but also really hard course.

I don't think I had planned to study computer science in college, but I did take a course my first quarter.

I ended up studying computer science in college at Stanford as my major, with a focus on artificial intelligence.

The way it worked for me, and the way many programs are structured, is that there is a core set of classes you need to take and then a set of elective classes or areas that you might have as a focus. For example, you may have a requirement to take "CS1" (Computer Science 1), "CS2," and "CS3" as your first three classes. My CS1 class was the class I got credit for in high school, in Java. The CS2 class was in C++. And the CS3 class was in C. You would also take probability courses and algorithms courses.

Beyond that, there were various focus areas. Some of them included artificial intelligence, database, graphics, systems, theory, and human-computer interaction. But that's just where I did it, and other colleges structure it in various ways.

At MIT, you'll take some intro courses but also algorithms courses, programming courses, AI courses, and theory courses. At Harvard, you'll have intro courses, math courses, and some breadth courses, which could include economics, hardware, networks, programming languages, or systems. At the University of Illinois, the computer science major includes the core classes with data structures, probability, intro to computer science, and algorithms and have focus areas in software foundations, algorithms, and intelligence and big data.

So, these programs have a common structure of core classes, advanced classes, and focus areas. That's a bit of what you would expect in a computer science major. Lots of these programs have slightly different naming conventions but, in essence, are deeper versions of concepts we introduced in this book, from programming languages to artificial intelligence to algorithms.

Coding Bootcamps

Another area within the coding education space that has popularized in the last few years is the idea of a coding bootcamp. These are intensive, job-oriented programs preparing people for jobs in computer science and related fields, often software engineering. There are now lots of coding bootcamps (many have come and gone), and there are various models. They can range in time, maybe from a couple of months to two years. But in general, they are shorter, intensive programs. Students going to coding bootcamps could be adults looking for career transitions or others trying to break into computer science. These are often more job-focused than a computer science degree at a traditional university but play an important part in the coding education landscape.

These programs often partner with employers and have job services—training, helping with preparing a resume, a portfolio, and interviewing. There are pros and cons, but often, these cost less than many colleges. Bootcamps have received criticism for not covering things as in-depth as a university or being too job-focused. I think they serve a function in the market where there are lots of opportunities in coding, and these provide an intensive way to get started with them.

These are a lot of work for students; it's no walk in the park. Though it might not cost the same as college, they still can be very expensive. There are part-time and full-time programs, but the full-time programs are a lot of work.

They will often go through curricula on popular programming languages, like Python or JavaScript (and possibly libraries or frameworks), but these often change rapidly.

Job Opportunities in Computer Science

Right now, coding is an in-demand job skill. There are about 4.5 million people who work in computing-related fields in the United States, about 1.8 million as software developers. There are projected to be around 600,000 job opportunities in the next ten years just in the US, and these opportunities are growing faster than many other jobs. There are only around 65,000 computer science graduates in the US each year. The numbers just reiterate what we see to be true—understanding and working with technology is becoming increasingly more important across industries.

So, what are these jobs, and what do programmers do?

One job that we have at our company is software engineer. Alternatively, this job could also be called programmer, coder, or a software developer. Generally, these are the same job but may have different names. This job is for people who are actually doing the coding day-to-day and building the application, website, or whatever else it is that needs to get built. They are taking ideas to be built (or designs, or descriptions of projects) and coding them up. They are testing them, making sure they work, and reviewing the documentation to find what they need. They are debugging, solving problems, and making fixes when it doesn't work. They are reviewing the code from other people. It's a challenging job that requires lots of time and focused work.

But there are lots of other jobs related to computer science.

You could be a data analyst or data scientist, working with building and analyzing data.

You could work with databases. You could work in cybersecurity with information security or on networks.

You could be a specific type of programmer, like a web developer or mobile app developer, or focus on the design side and be a designer. You could work with artificial intelligence, be a machine learning scientist, and build algorithms. You could work on the academic side and be a researcher. You could build the hardware and be a hardware engineer.

And there are so many more. And it's changing all the time. But what I think, mainly, is, If the software and robots are coming to take the jobs, which could be true, the most defensible skill today is coding. You'd rather be able to code the robots than have them program or tell you what to do. Even if people speculate today that computers will be able to write all the programs and reach a superintelligent state...the last line of defense will be the programmers.

Applications of Computer Science

Code is everywhere today. Sometimes you just need to know where to look. You'll find technology in every industry, and code is the language that powers that technology. It may be old or new or in all sorts of programming languages and tools, but the humming world of computing needs someone to program it.

You'll find coding in health and medicine. The medical records that people use today are being digitized with electronic medical records. Many of the machines that are used in healthcare have a programming element.

In biology, there is a whole field of biocomputation. With biocomputation, we are combining data and biology. How does the human genome work? How are we discovering and researching new diseases?

Economics is powered by code. You gather data about what is out there and research and build simulations.

Aerospace needs code. Code is written to power systems that send astronauts to space, launch satellites, send people to the moon, and send rovers to Mars.

But it just keeps going. The financial industry uses code. The stock market has lots of programs, and high-frequency traders write algorithms that trade. Banking is online, and banks have websites.

People to Know

How did we get to the moon? We needed code to make that happen too. Margaret Hamilton, who was a pioneer of computer science and coined the term "software engineering," oversaw the development of the software that helped the Apollo mission put people on the moon.

Some early Black women pioneers in space and aeronautics are featured in the movie *Hidden Figures*, including Dorothy Vaughan, Katherine Johnson, and Mary Jackson.

Katherine Johnson pioneered using computers to perform flight calculations, calculating the trajectory for space flight for the first moon landing. In 1958, Mary Jackson became NASA's first Black female engineer. Dorothy Vaughan learned and taught other programmers FORTRAN to help with new computations.

Pick your favorite app. If you use Facebook, Instagram, Snapchat, Twitter, TikTok, whatever it is—that app was coded. They coded the interface and have built social networks that today connect billions of people.

Pick your favorite game. It could be a mobile game or on a gaming platform, but they are coding the characters, the logic, the levels, and everything.

Find your favorite movie. The special effects, the animations, whatever it is: that is code. There is software, and someone could build it and the next version of it—it could be you.

The education field uses code as well.

At CodeHS, we make blended learning online education software tools. We make the curriculum accessible to millions of students and software for teachers to manage their classes. Blended learning allows more students to learn all over the world. I've been able to see firsthand what you can do with coding. Learning to code enabled me to start CodeHS, an education technology company, and we've been applying these skills every day as we build and scale our business. I could never have imagined what you can do with coding the first time I created an HTML website.

10
Under the Hood

100101010110100010101010000101001010010101010101010101011101010110010101001010101010100101010010101

Part of what coding allows you to do is go "under the hood" to demystify the world of technology. You've been doing some of that already, with the "Try It" challenges in this book and any visits you've made to the book's website, *readwritecodebook.com*. Here are a few more ways you can get started going under the hood to see how things work for yourself.

Under the Hood

Explore the Terminal

You know how in a movie, when there is a hacker, there is a computer screen with text scrolling through—what is that? That's usually the Terminal. If you are on a Mac, open up the program called "Terminal."

This is a way to run commands or programs on the computer that might not use a visual interface like other apps that you have.

Try to type:

```
python
```

This opens up a Python shell.

Then, see what you can do there. Type in a math problem:

```
18 * 101
```

Type in a print function:

```
print("Hello")
```

If you exit out or open a new window, type:

```
ls
```

This lists the files in your current directory.
Type:

```
cd
```

That lets you change directories.
For example, if I type:

```
cd Desktop
```

That lets me go to my Desktop. Then, if I type `ls` again, I can see the files on my Desktop.

There are a lot more! But go try to explore it.

View Page Source

Go to the website for this book (*readwritecodebook.com*) or any website. Then, right-click and select "View Page Source" or type the shortcut command + option + U.

This opens up the source for the website you are on.

You can see the actual HTML, CSS, and JavaScript that is running to make your page work.

Open the Inspector

Visit any page, like the site for this book or Google or whatever you want. Then, right-click on the page and select "Inspect." This opens the web inspector. From here, you can see the interactive HTML elements that make up the web page and try changing them around. You can also explore the CSS styles.

You can open up a JavaScript console and try entering JavaScript.

You can go to the Network tab to see the HTTP requests that are being made for this page.

Write a Program

Go to *readwritecodebook.com* and explore the examples. You can see links to start writing a program on CodeHS. You'll get an easy environment to write a program in and see what it does.

Google It!

If you want to figure out how something works, or why something is broken, or how to use a command in a programming language, or how to understand more about a topic in AI or the internet—google it! There are lots more resources to see, and you can often go look at the code directly.

How This Book Website Was Made

To make the website for this book, I wrote the pages in HTML on my computer, using the Sublime Text web editor. I managed the code using a Git repository and had a page on GitHub to manage it. I pushed the code to my personal web server using a script that moves the files into the right directory, so you could see it when you visited the page.

Any of the interactive coding programs are run on CodeHS, which you can also try for yourself.

What Can You Do Next?

Now that you've made it almost to the end of the book, hopefully, the world of coding makes a bit more sense. There is a lot to it. But the best way to understand things more is really to try it, experiment, and see how it all works for yourself. Here are a few projects you can do to learn more. You can find more information on these challenges at *readwritecodebook.com*.

Complete a Coding Course

A great place to start is to complete a coding or computer science course. What type of course you do will depend on your age, your previous experience, and your goals for taking the course. If you are in middle school or high school, see if you have a computer science course offered at your school. A good place to start is an introductory course. You may also have a coding club.

If you are at college, see what computer science courses are offered there. There are online courses and in-person courses, so you can find what works best for you.

On CodeHS, we have lots of courses, geared for students and teachers, that can be taken with a full classroom and teacher or on your own.

If you are an adult and not going to take full-time or part-time classes, you may want to look at online courses—but make sure to find an accountability mechanism to help keep you on track!

Make Your Own Website

I really learned a lot about coding from building websites. I think building websites lets you explore various parts of the web and understand how it works. Also, if you make your own site and can see how that whole process works, a lot of the pieces will come together. See if you can buy your own domain name, write your first page in HTML and CSS, get it all online, and make an update. The first website you make will probably be very basic, and that is okay! You can build it out from there.

Learn about One Future Technology

We've introduced a few new technologies in this book, but we only scratched the surface. Did you find that self-driving cars sparked your interest? Or did you want to learn more about cryptocurrencies or artificial intelligence? Or something even newer you found out about? See if you can find a few news articles, a few research papers, or a few companies working on the problem. What are people working on, and what are possible ways the technology can go in the next year, five years, or ten years?

Check If Your School Teaches Computer Science

If you are a student, see if you can take a coding or computer science class at your school. If you are a teacher, you can start to run a class or go to a professional development session. What we do at CodeHS is help schools launch and develop these programs by giving the full curriculum, teacher resources, software, and training.

Explore the *readwritecodebook.com* Website

If you haven't done it yet, visit the *readwritecodebook.com* website and explore lots of the programs. You can write a Karel program, a Python program, a JavaScript program, and more.

11
Conclusion

We started with 1s and 0s. Those are the building blocks of the digital world. The 1s and 0s are the bits—the on-and-off switches, yes/no, true/false, and transistors—that the rest is built upon.

You take the 1s and 0s—that's a bit—together in groups of 8—and that's a byte. You take more of those, and you use bytes to store and interpret data. That could be characters, or text, or numbers. You take an image that is made up of pixels, each represented by bits and bytes. You store lots of files—they could be photos, songs, or anything else—and you move from bytes to kilobytes to megabytes to gigabytes.

You start on the hardware side, moving from a transistor to the computer memory to the CPU, which is the brain of the computer. The computer doesn't know much, but it can go, one by one, through instructions and go through them billions of times in a second.

But it's hard to program 1s and 0s or work directly in the machine language. So, there are higher-level programming languages, or ways to give instructions to a computer. There are lots of languages for lots of purposes, some for various domains. There is JavaScript, which is a popular language on the web, and Python, and C, and C++, and many more.

In a programming language, there are a few fundamentals. It's about giving instructions to a computer, just like giving commands to a dog, like Karel. It builds up, and you teach the dog a new trick, you teach the dog a new function, and you build up reusable components that you can use to write more complex programs.

With a programming language, you have commands, which are your basic instructions. You have the ability to repeat them with for loops and while loops. You have the ability to make decisions to do one thing or another, depending on other factors, using if statements and if/else statements. You bring these together as control structures, which determine the flow of your program. And you create reusable components like functions you can use. You build these functions into larger programs, or into apps, or into websites—or whatever you can come up with.

As you take on larger problems, you develop an algorithm, a step-by-step process for accomplishing a task. You may outline your algorithm in pseudocode, basically outlining it in plain English but making clear the steps and the process, which you then can translate more easily into code. Algorithms are what let computers solve more complex problems. You can use them to search, or sort, or solve a maze, or plan a trip.

The internet brings computing and technology to the world, and it's built on a few big ideas. It's a distributed system, made up of lots of computers. You can access it through your web browser, typing in a domain name or URL to bring up a web page. These web pages are built with HTML for the structure, CSS for the design, and

JavaScript for the interactivity and the logic. You make a request for the website, and you get a response back from the server. Now, these servers are hosted all over the world, and these servers make up the cloud. A server is just someone else's computer, and the cloud is what you get when you put that all together. This means that the data you have is saved somewhere else, so you can log in and access it from anywhere.

And while this technology has enabled so much—powerful applications, new businesses, ways to connect people—there are some predicaments brought on by the new technology that we still have to deal with as a society. With the spread of free information and search is also the problem of combating misinformation and improving critical thinking. With the increased accessibility of free applications and ability to use them from anywhere is also the increase in data collection, privacy issues, and surveillance.

And then there are the hacks. The hacks that come more and more frequently show the need for cybersecurity and making these systems more secure from bad actors. You can still do a lot to improve your own security online. Make sure to learn and be aware of security issues. To keep your logins and passwords safe, you should have separate passwords on separate accounts. Your passwords should be longer (at least ten characters) to protect against a brute force attack and shouldn't be simple dictionary words. But they can be phrases or rules that make them easier to remember and still more secure. You should be aware of the types of attacks, like phishing—people trying to get you to give your login information to them or take over your accounts. You should set up two-factor authentication wherever possible, which means something you have and something you know, so it's harder to get into your accounts. And if you are interested in experimental applications of cryptography and computer science, you can explore Bitcoin, Ethereum, cryptocurrency, and blockchains.

And the programs and computers are getting smarter. While some warn of a coming robot apocalypse or a superintelligent future, there are certainly more moderate forms of AI to know. AI is about computers learning, making decisions, and trying to simulate human behavior. Often, under the hood, the computer isn't "smart" but just applying a probabilistic model to a dataset to optimize a function. There is ongoing work for general intelligence, or AI, that can do what a human can do and pass the Turing Test. This is an area of lots of work and already lots of applications, from spam to movie recommendations to your news feed.

So, how can you learn about this? Well, you have already started; congrats! Try going under the hood to explore, test out the Terminal, view the source, inspect a website, and write a program. There are now more courses in school, out of school, and online. Learning the fundamentals is a great place to start. Finding your interest areas to find connections between code is a great way to continue. One of the first websites I made was actually for a comedy newspaper in high school. I could combine my interest in comedy writing with coding. But the sky is the limit. And, while lots of this book is about the fundamentals, the cutting edge changes fast. Who knows what will be part of the world of computing in the next year or in five, ten, twenty, or fifty years?

This is the way things are going. Code isn't a language on the side anymore; it's the engine behind technology. And with reading and writing, it's a skill to know that makes up a basic part of literacy today. Just like the printing press transformed access to reading and writing and basic literacy, computers and the internet are transforming the access and requirement to know coding as part of the world of technology.

So, what will you code next?

Acknowledgments

It's been a big project to turn this idea into a book, and I want to thank many people who helped along the way.

I want to thank my family for being supportive and encouraging me to write this book.

To all the early readers of the manuscript, thank you for your advice. Thanks to my brother Zach Keeshin for being the first early reader of the book manuscript. Thanks also to Evelyn Hunter, John Kelly, and Elliot Babchick for reading drafts and offering your insight and perspective to help make this a better book. Thanks to Zach Galant, my business partner and co-founder at CodeHS, for collaborating with me for over a decade.

To the team at Scribe, thank you for helping to make the book a reality and helping me throughout the writing, editing, and publishing process. Thanks to Colleen Kapklein for your insights and feedback in editing, thanks to Natalie Aboudaoud for helping to navigate the publishing process, and thanks to Rachael Brandenburg and Michael Nagin for helping to create a great cover design. Thanks to the QA team, Amanda Woodward, Areil Sutton, Holly Gorman, and Lisa Caskey, for your diligent review of the manuscript. Thanks to the other Scribe writers who helped keep me motivated along the way.

To all the current, past, and future members of the CodeHS team: thank you. I appreciate that you've helped create an organization and product that can truly empower students and teachers, and I'm appreciative of what we've accomplished together over the last eight years. This book is only possible because of the work we've done together.

To my teachers, computer science teachers, and professors, thank you for helping to share your excitement and passion for teaching and learning.

To all the teachers who have taught with CodeHS: thank you. You are the ones connecting with students and inspiring them, and I hope this book can be a resource to you wherever you are on your computer-science-teaching journey.

About the Author

Jeremy Keeshin is the CEO and co-founder of CodeHS, the leading coding education platform for schools used by millions of students. He is an expert in computer science education and education technology, and he has visited hundreds of schools all over the world. Prior to starting CodeHS, he taught computer science at Stanford. Keeshin is an avid comedy fan, juggler, and traveler. He lives in Chicago.

jeremykeeshin.com